The Neter Sesen
(The Shat Sila Ma'at -The Nesu Enderase)

TM

Interpretation and Commentary

By

Ras Nahmir Amun

**VOLUME 1**

# The Shat-Sila Ma'at

Interpreted by Ras-Nahmir Amun

.

Some parts of this book mention other authors and research works and are strictly used for
a refrence guide and a clearly marked, where it appears.

ISBN - 978-0-9885163-1-1

Secound Edition

# Table of Contents

## The Shat-Sila Ma'at

*(The Books of Wisdom and Order)*

## Forward

In ancient Kemit (Egypt) Tehuti is credited with the invention of writing, literature, law, Faith, Mathematics, Science and Astronomy. It could be said he represents the embodiment of these attributes and or the discipline of education and its application. It is said he is the author of all the text compiled herein entrusted to his priesthood to help civilize and develop mankind that they may know themselves by knowing the Earth, the Heavens and the forces that move and shape the universe; and give Glory to Amen.

Much of the three great religions Judaism, Christianity, and Islam, owe there beginnings and source to the Nile valley civilizations and the texts compiled herein. Be it the 12 commandments from the "42 Divine Principles", to the Lords Prayer from the "Emerald Tablet", to the declaration of the Prophet Muhammad to Muslims to seek knowledge and wisdom liken onto Imhotep seeking "Sense and Understanding." From giving salat (prayer) to the burning of incenses and to holidays, and countless other comparisons, much was borrowed, taken and stolen from the Nile valley civilizations cultures, sciences and faiths; they used it to civilize themselves through blending it with their culture and practices but defiled it by abusing others, forcing them to submit and convert to their foreign culture disguised within their Spurious Religions; instead of sharing the Primary way of the universal principals.

Presented here are these universal principles, written down many thousands of years ago. Translated from Hieroglyphic, Coptic, Greek, Syriac, Latin, Arabic, Germanic, Old English to English. Many hands have translated these sacred texts; I have only edited the body of information from the Greek representations to the original Kemetic and slightly adjusted the grammar for the modern English language. With the exception of the fore mentioned, nothing has been generally added or taken from the text compiled. I wish to provide the reader with a complete and concise manuscript.

Before the burning of the library of Ra-Kedet (Alexandria) many manuscripts of knowledge and history lay in Kemet; of all places in the world most people came there to learn. These are not the only manuscripts to survive, many are hidden, lost, integrated or overlooked. These compiled were seen as a gateway to a clearer **understanding** of life and salvation.

Hotep, Ras Nahmir Amun

## The First Book. Heaven and Earth

1. My Son, write this first Book, both for Humanity's sake, and for Piety towards Amen.

2. For there can be no Faith more true or just, than to know the things that are; and to acknowledge thanks for all things, to the one that made them, which thing I will not cease continually to do.

3. What then should a man do, O Father, to lead his life well, seeing there is nothing here true?

4. Be Pious and Religious, O my Son, for he that does so, is the best and highest Philosopher; and without Philosophy, it is impossible ever to attain to the height and exactness of Piety or Faith.

5. But he that will learn and study the things that are, and how they are ordered and governed, and by whom and for what cause, or to what end, will acknowledge thanks to the Workman as to a good Father, an excellent Nurse and a faithful Steward, and he that gives thanks will be Pious or Religious, and he that is Religious will know both where the truth is, and what it is, and learning that, he will be yet more and more Religious.

6. For never, O Son, will or can that Soul which while it is in the Body lightens and lifts up itself to know and comprehend that which is Good and True, slide back to the contrary; for it is infinitely enamored thereof and forget all Evils; and when it has learned and known its Father and progenitor it can no more separate or depart from that Good.

7. And let this, O Son, be the end of Faith and Piety; whereto when you have once arrived, you will both live well, and die blessedly, while your Soul is not ignorant whether it must return and fly back again. For this only, O Son, is the way to the Truth, which our Progenitors traveled in; and by which, making their Journey, they at length attained to the Good. It is a Venerable way, and plain, but hard and difficult for the Soul to go in that is in the Body.

8. For first must it war against its own self, and after much Strife and Dissention it must be overcome of one part; for the Contention is of one against two, while it flies away and they strive to hold and detain it. But the victory of both is not like; for the one has to that which is Good, but the other is a neighbor to the things that are Evil; and that which is Good, desires to be set at Liberty; but the things that are Evil, Love Bondage and Slavery.

9. And if the two parts be overcome, they become quiet, and are content to accept of it as their Ruler; but if the one be overcome of the two, it is by them led and carried to be punished by its being and continuance here. This is, O Son, the Guide in the way that leads here for you must first forsake the Body before your end, and get the victory in this harsh and stressful life, and when you have overcome, return. But now, O my Son, I will by Heads run through the things that are; understand what I say, and remember what you hear.

10. All things that are, are moved; only that which is not, is unmovable.

11. Every Body is changeable.

12. Not every Body is dissolvable.

13. Some Bodies are dissolvable.

14. Every living thing is not mortal.

15. Not every living thing is immortal.

16. That which may be dissolved is also corruptible.

17. That which abides always is unchangeable.

18. That which is unchangeable is eternal.

19. That which is always made is always corrupted.

20. That, which is made but once, is never corrupted, neither becomes any other thing.

21. First, Amen; Secondly, the World; Thirdly, Man.

22. The World for Man, Man for Amen.

23. Of the Soul, that part which is Sensible is mortal, but that which is Reasonable is immortal.

24. Every essence is immortal.

25. Every essence is unchangeable.

26. Everything that is, is double.

27. None of the things that are stand still.

28. Not all things are moved by a Soul, but everything that is, is moved by a Soul.

29. Everything that suffers is Sensible; everything that is Sensible suffered.

30. Everything that is sad rejoices also, and is a mortal living Creature.

31. Not everything that is happy is also sad, but is an eternal living thing.

32. Not every Body is sick; every Body that is sick is dissolvable.

33. The Mind in Amen.

34. Reasoning (or disputing or discoursing) in Man.

35. Reason in the Mind.

36. The Mind is void of suffering.

37. No thing in a Body is true.

38. All that is immaterial is void of Lying.

4

39. Everything that is made is corruptible.

40. Nothing good on Earth, nothing evil in Heaven.

41. Amen is good, Man is evil.

42. Good is voluntary, or of its own accord.

43. Evil is involuntary or against its will.

44. The Neter choose good things, as good things.

45. Time is a Divine thing.

46. Law is Humane.

47. Malice is the nourishment of the World.

48. Time is the Corruption of Man.

49. Whatever is in Heaven is unalterable.

50. All on Earth is alterable.

51. Nothing in Heaven is servant, nothing on Earth is free.

52. Nothing unknown in Heaven, nothing known on Earth.

53. The things on Earth communicate not with those in Heaven.

54. All things in Heaven are without blame; all things upon Earth are subject to Reprehension.

55. That which is immortal, is not mortal; that which is mortal is not immortal.

56. That which is sown, is not always produced; but that which is produced always, is sown.

57. For a dissolvable Body, there is two Times, one from sowing to generation, one from generation to death.

58. Of an everlasting Body, the time is only from the Generation.

59. Dissolvable Bodies are increased and diminished.

60. Dissolvable matter is altered into contraries; to wit, Corruption and Generation, but Eternal matter into itself, and it's like.

61. The Generation of Man is Corruption; the Corruption of Man is the beginning of Generation.

62. That which off-springs or produces another, is itself an offspring or produced by another.

63. Of things that are, some are in Bodies, some in their Ideas.

64. Whatever things belong to operation or working, are in a Body.

65. That which is immortal, partakes not of that which is mortal.

66. That which is mortal, comes not into a Body immortal, but that which is immortal, comes into that which is mortal.

67. Operations or Workings are not carried upwards, but descend downwards.

68. Things on Earth do nothing to advantage those in Heaven, but all things in Heaven do profit and advantage the things on Earth.

69. Heaven is capable and a fit receptacle of everlasting Bodies, the Earth of corruptible Bodies.

70. The Earth is brutal; the Heaven is reasonable or rational.

71. Those things that are in Heaven are subjected or placed under it, but the things on Earth, are placed on it.

72. Heaven is the first Element.

73. Providence is Divine Order.

74. Necessity is the Minister or Servant of Providence.

75. Fortune is the carriage or effect of that which is without Order; the Idol of operation, a lying fantasy or opinion.

76. What is Amen? The immutable or unalterable Good.

77. What is Man? An unchangeable Evil.

78. If you perfectly remember these Heads, you cannot forget those things which in more words I have largely expounded to you; for these are the Contents or Summary of them.

79. Avoid all Conversation with the multitude or common People, for I would not have you subject to Envy, much less to be ridiculous to the many.

80. For the like always takes to itself that which is like, but the unlike never agrees with the like; such Discourses as these have very few Auditors, and perhaps very few will have, but they have something peculiar to themselves.

81. They do rather sharpen and whet evil men to their maliciousness, therefore it is necessary to avoid the multitude and be cautious of them as not understanding the virtue and power of the things that are said.

82. How do you mean, O Father?

83. Therefore, O Son, the whole Nature and Composition of those living things called Men, is very prone to Maliciousness, and is very familiar, and as it were nourished with it, and therefore is delighted with it. Now this creature if it will come to learn or know, that the world was once made, and all things are done according to Providence and Necessity, Destiny, or Fate, bearing Rule over all: Will he not be much worse than himself.

84. Despising the whole because it was made. And if he may lay the cause of evil upon Fate or Destiny, he will never hold back from doing any evil work.

85. This is why we must look warily to such kind of people, that being in ignorance, they may be less evil for fear of that which is hidden and kept secret.

## The Second Book. "The Divine Sesen."

1. My thoughts being once seriously busied about the things that are, and my Understanding lifted up, all my bodily Senses being exceedingly holding back, as it is with them that are very heavy of sleep, by reason either of fullness of meat, or of physical labor.

2. I thought I saw one of an exceeding great stature and an infinite greatness call me by my name, and say to me, "What would you Hear and See? Or what would you Understand, to Learn, and Know!"

3. Then I said, " Who are You?"

4. "I am," quote he, "Sesen, the mind of the Great Lord, the most Mighty and absolute Emperor: I know what you wish to have, and I am always present with you."

5. Then I said, "I wish to learn the Things that art, and understand the Nature of them and know Amen."

6. "How?" said he. I answered, "That I would gladly hear." Then he, "Have me again in your mind, and whatever you wish to learn, I will teach you."

7. When he had said so, he was changed in his Idea or Form and straightaway in the twinkling of an eye, all things were opened to me: and I saw an infinite Sight, all things were become light, both sweet and exceedingly pleasant; and I was wonderfully delighted in seeing it.

8. But after a little while, there was a darkness made in part, coming down obliquely, fearful and hideous, which seemed to me to be changed into a Certain Moist Nature, unspeakably troubled, which yielded a smoke as from fire; and from where proceeded a voice unutterable, and very mournful, but inarticulate, so that it seemed to have come from the Light.

9. Then from that Light, a certain Holy Word joined itself to Nature, and

9

out flew the pure and unmixed Fire from the moist Nature upward on high; it is exceeding Light, and Sharp, and Operative also. And the Air which was also light, followed the Spirit and mounted up to Fire (from the Earth and the Water) so that it seemed to hang and depend upon it.

10. And the Earth and the Water stayed by themselves so mingled together, that the Earth could not be seen for the Water, but they were moved, because of the Spiritual Word that was carried upon them.

11. Then said Sesen to me, "Do you understand this Vision, and what it meant?"

12. "I will know," said I. Then he said, "I am that Light, the Mind, your Amen, who am before that Moist Nature that appeared out of Darkness, and that Bright and Lightful Word from the Mind is the Son of Amen."

13. "How is that?" I asked. "Therefor," replied he, "Understand it, That which in you Sees and Hears, the Word of the Lord, and the Mind, the Father, Amen, Differed not One from the Other, and the Unison of these is Life.

14. Tehuti: "I thank you," Sesen: "But first conceive well the Light in your mind and know it."

15. When he had said so, for a long time I looked steadfastly one upon the other, so that I trembled at his Idea or Form.

16. But when he nodded to me, I saw in my mind the Light that is innumerable, and the truly indefinite Ornament or World; and that the Fire is comprehended or contained in or by a most great Power, and constrained to keep its stature.

17. These things I understood, seeing the word of Sesen; and when I was mightily amazed, he said again to me, "Have you seen in your mind that Archetypal Form, which was before the endless and Infinite Beginning?" So Sesen said to me.

18. "But where," asked I, "or of what are the Elements of Nature made?"

19. Sesen: "Of the Will and Counsel of Amen; which taking the Word, and seeing the beautiful World and know the architect of it, and who so made this World, by the principles and vital Seeds or Soul-like productions of itself."

20. For the Mind being Amen, Male and Female, Life and Light, brought forth by his Word; another Mind, the Workman: Which being Amen of the Fire, and the Spirit, fashioned and formed seven other Governors, which in their Circles contain the Sensible World, whose Government or Disposition is called Fate or Destiny.

21. Straightaway the soul leaped out, or exalted itself front the downward born Elements of Amen, by the Word of Amen into the clean and pure Workmanship of Nature, and was united to the Workman's Mind, where it was produced; and so the downward born Elements of Nature were left without Reason, that they might be left as Matter.

22. But the Workman, Mind, together with the Word, containing the Circles and Whirling them about, turned round as a Wheel his own Workmanships, and suffered them to be turned from an indefinite Beginning to an undeterminable End; for they always begin where they end.

23. And the Circulation or running round of these, as the Mind wills, out of the lower or downward-born Elements brought forth unreasonable or brutal creatures, for they had no reason, in the Air flying things, and the Water such as to swim.

24. And the Earth and the Water were separated, either from the other, as the Mind would the body; and the Earth brought forth from herself such Living Creatures as she had, four-footed and creeping Beasts, wild and tame.

25. But the Father of all things, the Mind being Life and Light, brought forth Man, like to himself, whom he loved as his proper Birth, for he was all beautiful, having the Image of his Father.

26. For indeed Amen was exceedingly pleased of his own Form or Shape, and delivered to it all his own Workmanships. But he seeing and

11

understanding the Creation of the Workman in the whole, with needs also himself left to work, and so was separated from the Father, being in the sphere of Generation or operation.

27. Having all Power, he considered the Operations or Workmanships of the Seven; but they loved him, and every one made him partaker of his own Order.

28. And he learning diligently and understanding their Essence, and partaking in their nature, resolved to pierce and break through the Circumference of the Circles, and to understand the Power of him that sits upon the Fire.

29. And having already all power of mortal things, of the Living, and of the unreasonable Creatures of the World, stooped down and peeped through the Harmony, and breaking through the strength of the Circles, so showed and made manifest the downward-born Nature, the fair and beautiful Shape or Form of Amen.

30. Which when he saw, having in itself the insatiable Beauty and all the Operation of the Seven Governors, and the Form or Shape of Amen, he Smiled for love, as if he had seen the Shape or Likeness in the Water, or the shadow upon the Earth of the fairest Human form.

31. And seeing in the Water a shape, a shape like to himself in himself he loved it, and would cohabit with it; and immediately upon the resolution, ensuing the Operation, and brought forth the unreasonable Image or Shape.

32. Nature presently laying hold of what it so much loved, fully wrapped herself around it, and they were mingled, for they loved one another.

33. And for this cause, Man above all things that live on Earth, is double; Mortal because of his Body, and Immortal because of the substantial Man; for being immortal, and having power of all things, he yet suffers mortal things, and such as are subject to Fate or Destiny.

34. And therefore being; above all Harmony, he is made and become a servant to Harmony. And being Hermaphrodite, or Male and Female, and

watchful, he is governed by and subjected to a Father, that is both Male and Female and watchful.

35. After these things, I said: "You are my Mind and I am in love with Reason."

36. Then Sesen said, "This is the Mystery that to this day is hidden, and kept secret; for Nature being mingled with Man brought forth a Wonder most wonderful; for he having the Nature of the Harmony of the Seven, from him whom I told you, the Fire and the Spirit, Nature continued not, but forth with brought forth seven Men all Males and Females and sublime, or on high, according to the Natures of the Seven Governors."

37. "And after these things, O Sesen," I said, "I have now a great desire, and longing to hear, do not digress, or run out."

38. But he said, "Keep silent, for I have not yet finished the first speech."

39. Tehuti: "See, I am silent."

40. Sesen: "The Generation therefore of these Seven was after this manner, the Air being Feminine and the Water desirous of Copulation, took from the Fire its ripeness, and from the ether Spirit; and so Nature produced bodies after the Species and Shape of men."

41. And Man was made of Life and Light into Soul and Mind, of Life the Soul, of Light the Mind.

42. And so all the Members of the Sensible World, continued to the period of the end, bearing rule, and generating.

43. Hear now the rest of that speech, you so much desire to hear.

44. When that Period was fulfilled, the bond of all things was released and untied by the Will of Amen; for all living Creatures being Hermaphroditical, or Male and Female, were released and untied together with Man; and so the Males were apart by themselves and the Females likewise.

45. And straightaway Amen said to the Holy Word, Increase in Increasing, and Multiply in Multitude all you my Creatures and Workmanships. And let Him that is gifted with Mind, know Himself to be Immortal; and that the cause of Death is the Love of the Body, and let Him Learn all Things that are.

46. When he had said so, Providence by Fate and Harmony, made the mixtures, and established the Generations, and all things were multiplied according to their kind, and he that knew himself, came at length to the utmost and lowest good.

47. But he that through the Error of Love, loved the Body, accepted wandering in darkness, sensible, suffering the things of death.

48. Tehuti: "But why do they that are ignorant sin so much, that they should therefore be deprived of immortality."

49. Sesen: "You seem not to have understood what you have heard."

50. Tehuti: "Perhaps I seem so to you, but I both understand and remember them."

51. Sesen: "I am glad for your sake, if you understood them."

52. Tehuti: "Tell me, why are they worthy of death, that are in death?"

53. Sesen: "Because there goes a sad and depressing darkness before its Body; of which darkness is the moist Nature, of which moist Nature, the Body consisted in the sensible World, from where death is derived. Have you understood this right?"

54. Tehuti: "But why or how does he that understands himself, go or passes into Amen?"

55. Sesen: "That which the Word of Amen said, say I: Because the Father of all things consists of Life and Light, of which Man is made."

56. Tehuti: "You say it very well."

57. Sesen: "Amen and the Father are Light and Life, of which Man is made. If therefore you learn and believe yourself to be of the Life and Light, you will again pass into Life."

58. Tehuti: "But yet tell me more, O my Mind, how I will go into Life."

59. Sesen: "Amen says, let the Man gifted with a Mind, mark, consider, and know himself well."

60. Tehuti: "Do not all men have a mind?"

61. Sesen: "Be cautious what you say, for I the Mind come to men that are holy and good, pure and merciful, and that live piously and religiously; and my presence is a help to them. And instantly they know all things, and lovingly they beg for and win the favor of the Father; and blessing Him, they give Him thanks, and sing hymns to Him, being ordered and directed by filial Affection, and natural Love; And before they give up their Bodies to the death of them, they hate their Senses, knowing their Works and Operations.

62. "Rather I that am the Mind itself will not suffer the Operations or Works, which happen or belong to the body, to be finished and brought to perfection in them; but being the Porter and Door-keeper, I will prevent all access to the entrances of Evil, and cut off the thoughtful desires of filthy works.

63. "But to the foolish, and evil, and wicked, and envious and covetous, and murderous, and profane, I am far off giving place to the avenging Spirit, which applying to him the sharpness of fire, tormented such a man sensibly, and armed him the more to all wickedness, that he may obtain the greater punishment.

64. "And such a one never ceases, having unfulfillable desires and insatiable desires, and always fighting in darkness for the Spirit afflicts and torments him continually, and increasing the fire on him more and more."

65. Tehuti: "You have, O Mind, most excellently taught me all things, as I desired; but tell me moreover, after the return is made, what then?"

66. Sesen: "First of all, in the resolution of the material Body, the Body itself is given up to alteration, and the form which it had becomes invisible; and the idle manners are permitted and left to the Spirit, and the Senses of the Body return into their Fountains, being parts, and again made up into Operations.

67. "And Anger and Concupiscence go into the brutal or unreasonable Nature; and the rest strives upward by Harmony.

68. "And to the first Zone it gives the power it had of increasing and diminishing.

69. "To the second, the scheming or plotting of evils, and one effectual deceit or craft.

70. "To the third, the idle deceit of Concupiscence.

71. "To the fourth, the desire of Rule, and insatiable Ambition.

72. "To the fifth, profane Boldness, and reckless rashness of Confidence.

73. "To the sixth, Evil and ineffectual occasions of Riches.

74. "And to the seventh Zone, subtle Falsehood always lying in wait.

75. "And then being made naked of all the Operations of Harmony it comes to the eighth Nature, having its proper power, and sings praises to the Father with the things that are, and all they that are present rejoice, and congratulate the coming of it; and being made like to them with whom it converses, it hears also the Powers that are above the eighth Nature, singing praise to Amen in a certain voice that is peculiar to them.

76. "And then in order they return to the Father, and themselves deliver themselves to the powers, and becoming powers they are in Amen.

77. "This is the Good, and to them that know to be deified.

78. "Furthermore, why do you say, what rest, but that understanding all men,

you become a guide, and way-leader to them that are worthy; that the kind of Humanity or Mankind, may be saved by Amen!"

79. When Sesen had said so to me, he was mingled among the Powers.

80. But I giving thanks and blessing the Father of all things rose up, being enabled by him, and taught the Nature of the Nature of the whole and having seen the greatest sight or spectacle.

81. And I began to Preach to men, the beauty and fairness of Piety and Knowledge.

82. O you People, Men, born and made of the Earth, which have given Yourselves over to Drunkenness, and Sleep, and to the Ignorance of Amen, be Sober, and Cease your Surfeit, to which you are allured, and invited by Brutal and Unreasonable Sleep.

83. And they that heard me, come willingly and with one accord, and then I said further:

84. Why, O Men of the Off-spring of the Earth, why have you delivered Yourselves over to Death, having Power to Partake of Immortality; Repent and Change your Minds, you that have together Walked in Error, and have been Darkened in Ignorance.

85. Depart from that dark Light, be Partakers of Immortality, and Leave or Forsake Corruption.

86. And some of Them That Heard Me, mocking and scorning, went away and delivered themselves up to the way of death.

87. But others, casting themselves down before my feet, appealed to me that they might be taught; but I causing them to rise up, became a guide of mankind, teaching them the reasons how, and by what means they may be saved. And I sowed in them the words of Wisdom, and nourished them with Ambrosia Water of Immortality.

88. And when it was Evening, and the Brightness of the same began fully to go down, I commanded them to give thanks to Amen; and when they had finished their thanksgiving, everyone returned to his own lodging.

89. But I wrote in myself the bounty and beneficence of Sesen; and being filled with what I most desired, I was exceedingly glad.

90. For the sleep of the Body was the sober watchfulness of the mind; and the shutting of my eyes the true Sight, and my silence great with child and full of good; and the pronouncing of my words, the blossoms and fruits of good things.

91. And so came to pass or happened to me, which I received from my mind, that is, Sesen, the Lord of the Word; by which I became inspired by Amen with the Truth.

92. For which cause, with my Soul, and whole strength, I give praise and blessing unto Amen the Father.

93. Holy is Amen the Father of All Things.

94. Holy is Amen Whose Will is Performed and Accomplished by His Own Powers.

95. Holy is Amen, that Determined to be Known, and is Known of His Own, or Those that are His.

96. Holy are You, Who by Your Word has established all Things.

97. Holy are You of Whom all Nature is the Image.

98. Holy are You, Whom Nature has not Formed.

99. Holy are You, Who is Stronger than all Power.

100. Holy are You, Who is Greater than all Excellency.

101. Holy are You, Who is Better than all Praise.

102. Accept these Reasonable Sacrifices from a Pure Soul, and a Heart stretched out to You.

103. O You Unspeakable, Unutterable, to be praised with Silence!

104. I appeal to you, that I may never Err from the Knowledge of You, Look Mercifully upon Me, and Enable Me, and Enlighten with this Grace, those that are in Ignorance, the Brothers of my Kind, but Your Sons.

105. Therefore I Believe You, and Bear Witness, and go into the Life and Light.

106. Blessed are You, O Father, Your Man would be sanctified with You, as You have given Him all Power.

## The Third Book. "The Holy Sermon."

**1.** The glory of all things, Amen and that which is Divine, and the Divine Nature, the beginning of things that are.

2. Amen, and the Mind, and Nature, and Matter, and Operation, or Working and Necessity, and the End and Renovation.

3. For there were in the Chaos, an infinite darkness in the Abyss or bottom-less Depth, and Water, and a subtle Spirit intelligible in Power; and there went out the Holy Light, and the Elements were coagulated from the Sand out of the moist Substance.

4. And all the Neter distinguished the Nature full of Seeds.

5. And when all things were in terminated and unmade up, the light things were divided on high. And the heavy things were founded upon the moist sand, all things being terminated or Divided by Fire; and being sustained or hung up by the Spirit they were so carried, and the Heaven was seen in Seven Circles.

6. And the Neter were seen in their Ideas of the Stars, with all their Signs, and the Stars were numbered, with the Neter in them. And the Sphere was all lined with Air, carried about in a circular, motion by the Spirit of Amen.

7. And every Neter by his internal power, did that which was commanded him; and there were made four footed things, and creeping things, and such as live in the Water, and such as fly, and every fruitful Seed, and Grass, and the Flowers of all Greens, and which had sowed in themselves the Seeds of Regeneration.

8. As also the Generations of men to the knowledge of the Divine Works, and a lively or working Testimony of Nature, and a multitude of men, and the Dominion of all things under Heaven and the knowledge of good things, and to be increased in increasing, and multiplied in multitude.

9. And every Soul in flesh, by the wonderful working of the Neter in the Circles, to the beholding of Heaven, the Neter, Divine Works, and the Operations of Nature; and for Signs of good things, and the knowledg of the Divine Power, and to find out every cunning workmanship of good things.

10. So it begins to live in them, and to be wise according to the Operation of the course of the circular Neter; and to be resolved into that which will be great Monuments; and Remembrances of the cunning Works done upon Earth, leaving them to be read by the darkness of times.

11. And every generation of living flesh, of Fruit, Seed, and all Handicrafts, though they be lost, must of necessity be renewed by the renovation of the Neter, and of the Nature of a Circle, moving in number; for it is a Divine thing, that every world temperature should be renewed by nature, for in that which is Divine, is Nature also established.

## The Fourth Book. "The Key."

1. Yesterday's Speech, O Imhotep, I dedicated to you, this day's speech it is fit to dedicate to Ptah, because it is an Summary of those general speeches that were spoken to him.

2. Amen therefore, and the Father, and the Good, O Imhotep, have the same Nature, or rather also the same Act and Operation.

3. For there is one name or appellation of Nature and Increase which concerns things changeable, and another about things unchangeable, and about things unmovable, that is to say, Things Divine and Human; every one of which, himself will have so to be; but action or operation is of another thing, or elsewhere, as we have taught in other things, Divine and Human, which must here also be understood.

4. For his Operation or Act, is his Will, and his Essence, to Will all Things to be.

5. For what is Amen, and the Father, and the Good, but the Being of all things that yet are not, and the existence itself, of those things that are!

6. This is Amen, this is the Father, this is the Good, whereto no other thing is present or approaches.

7. For the World, and the Sun, which is also a Father by Participation, is not for all that equally the cause of Good, and of Life, to living Creatures; and if this be so, he is altogether constrained by the Will of the Good, without which it is not possible, either to be, or to be produced or made.

8. But the Father is the cause of his Children, who has a will both to sow and nourish that which is good by the Son.

9. For Good is always active or busy in making; and this cannot be in any other, but in him that takes nothing, and yet wills all things to be; for I will

22

not say, O Imhotep, making them; for he that makes is defective in much time, in which sometimes he makes not, as also of quantity and quality; for sometimes he makes those things that have quantity and quality and sometimes the contrary.

10. But Amen is the Father, and the Good, in being all things; for he both will be this, and is it, and yet all this for himself (as is true) in him that can see it.

11. For all things else are for this, it is the property of Good to be known; This is the Good, O Imhotep.

12. Imhotep: "You have filled us, O Father, with a sight both good and fair and the eye of my mind is almost become more holy by the sight or spectacle."

13. Tehuti: "I Wonder not at It, for the Sight of Good is not like the Beam of the Sun, which being of a fiery shining brightness, makes the eye blind by his excessive Light, that gazes upon it; rather the contrary, for it enlightens, and so much increases the light of the eye, as any man is able to receive the influence of this Intelligible clearness.

14. For it is more swift and sharp to pierce, an innocent or harmless creature, and full of immortality, and they that are capable and can draw any store of this spectacle, and sight do many times fall asleep from the Body, into this most fair and beautiful Vision. "

15. Imhotep: "I wish we also, O Father, could do so. "

16. Tehuti: "I wish we could, O Son; but for the present we are less intent to the Vision, and cannot yet open the eyes of our minds to behold the incorruptible, and incomprehensible Beauty of that Good; but then will we see it, when we have nothing at all to say of it.

17. For the knowledge of it, is a Divine Silence, and the rest of all the Senses; for neither can he that understands that understand anything else, nor he that sees that, see anything else, nor hear any other thing, nor in sum, move the Body.

18. For shining steadfastly upon and round about the whole Mind it enlightens all the Soul; and releasing it from the Bodily Senses and Motions, it draws it from the Body, and changes it fully into the Essence of Amen.

19.For it is Possible for the Soul, O Son, to be Deified while yet it Lodges in the Body of Man, if it Contemplate the Beauty of the Good."

20. Imhotep: "How do you mean deifying, Father!"

21. Tehuti: "There are differences, O Son, of every Soul."

22. Imhotep: "But how do you again divide the changes?"

23. Tehuti: "Have you not heard in the general Speeches, that from one Soul of the Universe, are all those Souls, which in all the world are tossed up and down, as it were, and severally divided? Of these Souls there are many changes, some into a more fortunate lives, and some quite contrary; for they which are of creeping things, are changed into those of watery things and those of things living in the water, to those of things living upon the Land; and Airy ones are changed into men, and human Souls, that lay hold of immortality, are changed into Spirits.

24. And so they go on into the Sphere or Region of the fixed Neter, for there are two choirs or companies of Neter, one of them that wander, and another of them that are fixed. And this is the most perfect glory of the Soul.

25. But the Soul entering into the Body of a Man, if it continues evil, will neither taste of immortality, nor is partaker of the good.

26. But being drawn back the same way, it returns into creeping things. And this is the condemnation of an evil Soul.

27. And the wickedness of a Soul is ignorance; for the Soul that knows nothing of the things that are, neither the Nature of them, nor that which is good, but is blinded, rushes and dashes against the bodily Passions, and unhappy as it is, not knowing itself, it serves strange Bodies, and evil ones, carrying the Body as a burden, and not ruling, but ruled. And this is the mischief of the Soul.

28. On the contrary, the virtue of the Soul is Knowledge; for he that knows is both good and religious, and already divine."

29. Imhotep: "But who is such a one, O Father!"

30. Tehuti: "He that neither speaks, nor hears many things; for he, O Son, that hears two speeches or hearings, fights in the shadow.

31. For Amen, and the Father, and Good, is neither spoken nor heard.

32. This being so in all things that are, are the Senses, because they cannot be without them.

33. But Knowledge differs much from Sense; for Sense is of things that overcome it, but Knowledge is the end of Sense.

34. Knowledge is the gift of Amen; for all Knowledge is divine but uses the Mind as an Instrument, as the Mind uses the Body.

35. Therefore both intelligible and material things go both of them into bodies; for, of contraposition, That is Setting One against Another, and Contrariety, all Things must Consist. And it is impossible it should be otherwise."

36. Imhotep: "Who therefore is this material Amen?"

37. Tehuti: "The fair and beautiful world, and yet it is not good; for it is material and easily passable, no, it is the first of all passable things; and the second of the things that are, and needy or wanting somewhat else. And it was once made and is always, and is ever in generation, and made, and continually makes, or generates things that have quantity and quality.

38. For it is moveable, and every material motion is generation; but the intellectual stability moves the material motion after this manner.

39. Because the World Is a Sphere, that is a Head, and above the head there is nothing material, as beneath the feet there is nothing intellectual.

40. The whole universe is material; The Mind is the head, and it is moved spherically, that is like a head.

41. Whatever therefore is joined or united to the Membrane or Film of this head, wherein the Soul is, is immortal, and as in the Soul of a made Body, have its Soul full of the Body; but those that are further from that Membrane, have the Body full of Soul.

42. The whole is a living creature, and therefore consist of material and intellectual.

43. And the World is the first, and Man the second living creature after the World; but the first of things that are mortal and therefore has whatever benefit of the Soul all the others have; and yet for all this, he is not only not good, but flatly evil, as being mortal.

44. For the World is not good as it is moveable; nor evil as it is immortal.

45. But man is evil, both as he is moveable, and as he is mortal.

46. But the Soul of Man is carried in this manner; The Mind is in Reason, Reason in the Soul, the Soul in the Spirit, the Spirit in the Body.

47. The Spirit being diffused and going through the veins, and arteries, and blood, both moves the living Creature, and after a certain manner bears it.

48. This is why some also have thought the Soul to be blood, being deceived in Nature, not knowing that first the Spirit must return into the Soul, and then the blood is congealed, the veins and arteries emptied, and then the living thing dies; And this is the death of the Body.

49. All things depend of one beginning, and the beginning depends of that which is one and alone.

50. And the beginning is moved, that it may again be a beginning; but that which is one, stands and abides, and is not moved.

51. There are therefore these three, Amen the Father, and the Good, the World and Man: Amen has the World, and the World has Man; and the World is the Son of Amen, and Man as it were the Offspring of the World.

52. For Amen is not ignorant of the World, but knows him perfectly, and will be known by him. This only is healthful to man; the Knowledge of Amen. This is the return of Heaven; by this only the Soul is made good, and not sometimes good, and sometimes evil, but of necessity Good."

53. Imhotep: "What do you mean, O Father?"

54. Tehuti: "Consider, O Son, the Soul of a Child, when as yet it has received no dissolution of its Body, which is not yet grown, but is very small; how then if it looks upon itself, it sees itself beautiful, as not having been yet spotted with the Passions of the Body, but as it were depending yet upon the Soul of the World.

55. But when the Body is grown and distracts the Soul it engenders Forget-fulness, and partakes no more of the Fair and the Good, and Forgetfulness is Evilness.

56. The same also happens to them that go out of the Body; for when the Soul runs back into itself the Spirit is contracted into the blood and the Soul into the Spirit; but the Mind being made pure, and free from these clothes; and being Divine by Nature, taking a fiery Body ranges abroad in every place, leaving the Soul to judgment, and to the punishment it has deserved."

57. Imhotep: "Why do you say, O Father, that the Mind is separated from the Soul, and the Soul from the Spirit? When even now you say the Soul was the Clothing or Apparel of the Mind, and the Body of the Soul."

58. Tehuti: "O Son, he that hears must co-understand and conspire in thought with him that speaks; yea, he must have his hearing swifter and sharper than the voice of the speaker.

59. The disposition of these Clothes or Covers, is done in an Earthly Body; for it is impossible, that the mind should establish or rest itself, naked, and of

itself in an Earthly Body; neither is the Earthly Body able to bear such immortality; and therefore that it might suffer so great virtue the Mind compacted as it were, and took to itself the passable Body of the Soul, as a Covering or Clothing. And the Soul being also in some sort Divine uses the Spirit as her Minister and Servant, and the Spirit governs the living thing.

60. When therefore the Mind is separated, and departs from the earthly Body, presently it puts on its Fiery Coat, which it could not do having to dwell in an Earthly Body.

61. For the Earth cannot suffer fire, for it is all burned by a small spark; therefore is the water poured round about the Earth, as a Wall or defense, to withstand the flame of fire.

62. But the Mind being the most sharp or swift of all the Divine Senses, and more swift than all the Elements, has the fire for its Body.

63. For the Mind which is the Workman of all uses the fire as his instrument in his Workmanship; and he that is the Workman of all, uses it to the making of all things, as it is used by man, to the making of Earthly things only; for the Mind that is upon Earth, void, or naked of fire, cannot do the business of men nor that which is otherwise the affairs of Amen.

64. But the Soul of Man, and yet not everyone, but that which is pious and religious, is Angelical and Divine. And such a Soul, after it is departed from the Body, having striven the strife of Piety, becomes either Mind or Amen.

65. And the strife of Piety is to know Amen, and to injure no Man, and this way it becomes Mind.

66. But an impious Soul abides in its own essence, punished of itself, and seeking an earthly and human Body to enter into.

67. For no other Body is capable of a Human Soul, neither is it lawful for a Man's Soul to fall into the Body of an unreasonable living thing; for it is the Law or Decree of Amen, to preserve a Human Soul from so great an insult and reprimand."

68. Imhotep: "How then is the Soul of Man punished, O Father; and what is its greatest torment?"

69. Tehuti: "Impiety, O my Son, for what Fire has so great a flame as it? Or what biting Beast does so tear the Body as it does the Soul.

70. Or do you not see how many evils the wicked Soul suffers, roaring and crying out, I am Burned, I am Consumed, I know not what to Say, or Do, I am Devoured, Unhappy Wretch, of the Evils that compass and lay hold on me; miserable that I am, I neither See nor Hear anything.

71. These are the voices of a punished and tormented Soul, and not as many; and you, O Son, think that the Soul going out of the Body grows brutal or enters into a Beast; which is a very great Error, for the Soul punished after this manner.

72. For the Mind, when it is ordered or appointed to get a fiery Body for the services of Amen, coming down into the wicked Soul, torments it with the whips of Sins, with which the wicked Soul being scourged, turns itself to Murders, and Contumelies, and Blasphemies, and devises Violences, and other things by which men are injured.

73. But into a pious Soul, the Mind entering, leads it into the Light of Knowledge.

74. And such a Soul is never satisfied with singing praise to Amen, and speaking well of all men; and both in words and deeds, always doing well in the Presence of her Father.

75. Therefore, O Son, we must give thanks, and pray that we may obtain a good mind.

76. The Soul therefore may be altered or changed into the better, but into the worse it is impossible.

77. But there is a communion of Souls, and those of Neter, communicate with those of men; and those of men, with those of Beasts.

29

78. And the better always take of the worse, Neter of Men, Men of brute Beasts, but Amen of all; for he is the best of all, and all things are less than he.

79. Therefore the World is subject to Amen, Man to the World and unreasonable things to Man.

80. But Amen is above all, and about all; and the beams of Amen are operations; and the beams of the World are Natures; and the beams of Man are Arts and Sciences.

81. And Operations do act by the World, and on man by the natural beams of the World, but Natures work by the Elements, and man by Arts and Sciences.

82. And this is the Government of the whole, depending on the Nature of the One, and piercing or coming down by the One Mind, than which nothing is more Divine, and more efficacious or operative; and nothing more uniting, or nothing is more One. The Communion of the Neter to Men, and of Men to Amen.

83. This is the Great Spirit, or blessed Soul that is fullest of it and unhappy Soul that is empty of it!"

84. Imhotep: "And why Father?"

83. Tehuti: "Know Son that which every Soul has the Good Mind; for of that it is we now speak, and not of that Minister of which we said before, that he was sent from the Judgment.

86. For the Soul without the Mind, can neither do, nor say anything; for many times the Mind flies away from the Soul, and in that hour the Soul neither sees nor hears, but is like an unreasonable thing; so great is the power of the Mind.

87. But neither broke it an idle or lazy Soul, but leaves such a one fastened to the Body, and by it pressed down.

88. And such a Soul, O Son, has no mind, which is why neither must such a one be called a Man.

89. For man is a Divine living thing and is not to be compared to any brute Beast that lives upon Earth, but to them that are above in Heaven, that are called Neter.

90. Rather, if we shall be bold to speak the truth, he that is a man indeed, is above them, or at least they are equal in power, one to the other; for none of the things in Heaven will come down upon Earth, and leave the limits of Heaven, but a man ascends up into Heaven, and measures it.

91. And he knows what things are on high, and what below, and learns all other things exactly.

92. And that which is the greatest of all, he leaves not the Earth, and yet is above; so great is the greatness of his Nature.

93. Which is why we must be bold to say, that an Earthly Man is a Mortal Amen, and that the Heavenly Amen is an Immortal Man.

94. Which is why, by these two are all things governed, the World and Man; but they and all things else, of that which is One."

**The Fifth Book.** The Seen and Unseen Amen.

1. This Discourse I will also make to you, O Imhotep, that you may not be ignorant of the more excellent Name of Amen.

2. But do contemplate in your Mind, how that which to many seems hidden and unmanifest, may be most manifest to you.

3. For it were not all, if it were apparent, for whatever is apparent, is generated or made; for it was made manifest, but that which is not manifest is forever.

4. For it needed not to be manifested, for it is always.

5. And he makes all other things manifest, being unmanifest as being always, and making other things manifest, he is not made manifest.

6. He himself is not made, yet in fantasy he fantasizes all things, or in appearance he makes them appear, for appearance is only of those things that are generated or made, for appearance is nothing but generation.

7. But he is that One, that is not made nor generated, is also unapparent and unmanifest.

8. But making all things appear, he appears in all and by all; but especially he is manifested to or in those things where himself lists.

9. You therefore, O Imhotep, my Son, pray first to the Lord and Father, and to the Alone and to the One from whom is one to be merciful to you, that you may know and understand so great a Amen; and that he would shine one of his beams on you In your understanding.

10. For only the Understanding sees that which is not manifest or apparent, as being itself not manifest or apparent; and if you can, O Imhotep, it will appear to the eyes of your Mind.

11. For the Lord, void of envy, appears through the whole world. You may see the intelligence, and take it in your hands, and contemplate the Image of Amen.

12. But if that which is in you, be not known or apparent to you, how will He in you be seen, and appear to you by the eyes?

13. But if you want to see him, consider and understand the Sun, consider the course of the Moon, consider the order of the Stars.

14. Who is he that keeps order? For all order is circumscribed or terminated in number and place.

15. The Sun is the greatest of the Bodies in heaven, to whom all the heavenly Bodies give place, as to a King and subjects; and yet he being such a one, greater than the Earth or the Sea, is content to suffer infinite lesser stars to walk and move above himself; whom does he fear, O Son?

16. Every one of these Stars that are in Heaven, do not make the like, or an equal course; who is it that has prescribed to every one, the manner and the greatness of their course!

17. This Sphere that turns round about its own self; and carries round the whole World with her, who possessed and made such an Instrument.

18. Who has set the Bounds to the Sea; who has established the Earth? For there is somebody, O Imhotep, that is the Maker and Lord of these things.

19. For it is impossible, O Son, that either place, or number, or measure, should be observed without a Maker.

20. For no order can be made by disorder or disproportion.

21. I wish it were possible for you, O my Son, to have wings, and to fly into the Air, and being taken up in the midst, between Heaven and Earth, to see the stability of the Earth, the fluidness of the Sea, the courses of the Rivers, the largeness of the Air, the sharpness or swiftness of the Fire, the motion of

33

the Stars; and the speediness of the Heaven, by which it goes round about all these.

22. O Son, what a happy sight it were, at one instant, to see all these, that which is unmovable moved, and that which is hidden appear and be manifest.

23. And if you want to and behold this Workman, even by mortal things that are on Earth, and in the deep. Consider, O Son, how Man is made and framed in the Womb; and examine diligently the skill and cunning of the Workman, and learn who it was that wrought and fashioned the beautiful and Divine shape of Man; Who circumscribed and marked out his eyes? Who bored his nostrils and ears? Who opened his mouth? Who stretched out and tied together his sinews? Who channeled the veins? Who hardened and made strong the bones? Who clothed the flesh with skin? Who divided the fingers and the joints? Who flatted and made broad the soles of the feet? Who dug the pores? Who stretched out the spleen, who made the heart like a Pyramid? Who made the Liver broad? Who made the eyes spongy, and full of holes? Who made the belly large and capacious? Who set to outward view the more honorable parts and hid the filthy ones?

24. See how many Arts in one Matter, and how many Works in one Superscription, and all exceedingly beautiful, and all done in measure, and yet all differing.

25. Who has made all these things? What Mother? What Father? Save only Amen that is not manifest! That made all things by his own Will.

26. And no man says that a statue or an image is made without a Carver or a Painter, and was this Workmanship made without a Workman? O great Blindness, O great Impiety, O great Ignorance.

27. Never, O Son Imhotep, can you deprive the Workmanship of the Workman, rather it is the best Name of all the Names of Amen, to call Him the Father of all, for so he is alone; and this is His Work to be the Father.

28. And if you want to force me to say anything more boldly, it is His Essence to be pregnant, or great with all things, and to make them.

29. And as without a Maker, it is impossible that anything should be made, so it is that He should not always be, and always be making all things in Heaven, in the Air, in the Earth, in the Deep, in the whole World, and in every part of the whole that is, or that is not.

30. For there is nothing in the whole World, that is not Himself both the things that are and the things that are not.

31. For the things that are, He has made manifest; and the things that are not, He has hid in himself.

32. This is Amen that is better than any name; this is He that is secret; this is He that is most manifest; this is He that is to be seen by the Mind; this is He that is visible to the eye; this is He that has no body; and this is He that has many bodies, rather there is nothing of any body, which is not He.

33. For He alone is all things.

34. And for this cause He has all Names, because He is the One Father; and therefore He has no Name, because He is the Father of all.

35. Who therefore can bless you, or give thanks for you, or to you.

36. Which way will I look, when I praise You? Upward? Downward? Outward? Inward?

37. For about You there is no manner, nor place, nor anything else of all things that are.

38. But all things are in You; all things from You, You give all things, and take nothing; for You have all things and there is nothing that You do not have.

39. When will I praise You, O Father; for it is neither possible to comprehend Your hour, nor Your time?

40. For what will I praise You? For what You have made, or for what You have not made? For those things You have manifested, or for those things You have hidden?

41. Why will I praise You as being of myself, or having anything of mine own, or rather being another's?

42. For You are what I am, You are what I do, You are what I say.

43. You are All Things, and there is Nothing Else You are not.

44. You are You, All that is Made, and all that is not Made.

45. The Mind that Understands.

46. The Father that Makes and Frames.

47. The Good that Works.

48. The Good that does All Things.

49. Of the Matter, the most subtle and slender part is Air, of the Air the Soul, of the Soul the Mind, of the Mind Amen.

## The Sixth Book. "That in Amen alone is Good"

**1. Good, O Imhotep, is in nothing but in Amen alone; or rather Amen Himself is the Good always.**

2. And if it be so, then must He be an Essence or Substance void of all motion and generation; but nothing is void or empty of Him.

3. And this Essence has about or in Himself a Stable, and firm Operation, wanting nothing, most full, and giving abundantly.

4. One thing is the Beginning of all things, for it gives all things; and when I name the Good, I mean that which is altogether and always Good.

5. This is present to none, but Amen alone; for He wants nothing, that He should desire to have it, nor can anything be taken from Him; the loss of which may grieve Him; for sorrow is a part of evilness.

6. Nothing is stronger than He, that He should be opposed by it; nor nothing equal to Him, that He should be in love with it; nothing unheard of to be angry, with nothing wiser to be envious at.

7. And none of these being in His Essence, what remains, but only the Good?

8. For as in this, being such an Essence, there is none of the evils; so in none of the other things shall the Good be found.

9. For in all other things, are all those other things, as well in the small as the great; and as well in the particulars as in this living Creature the greater and mightiest of all.

10. For all things that are made or generated are full of Passion, Generation itself being a Passion; and where Passion is there is not the Good; where the Good is, there is no Passion; where it is day, it is not night, and where it is night, it is not day.

11. Why it is impossible, that in Generation should be the Good, but only in that which is not generated or made.

12. Yet as the Participation of all things is in the Matter bound, so also of that which is Good. After this manner is the World good, as it makes all things, and in the part of making or doing it is Good, but in all other things not good.

13. For it is passable, and movable, and the Maker of passable things.

14. In Man also the Good is ordered (or Takes Denomination) in comparison of that which is evil; for that which is not very evil, is here good; and that which is here called Good, is the least particle, or proportion of evil.

15. It is impossible therefore, that the Good should be here pure from Evil; for here the Good grows Evil, and growing Evil, it does not still act in accordance with Good; and not acting in accordance with Good it becomes Evil.

16. Therefore in Amen alone is the Good, or rather Amen is the Good.

17. Therefore, O Imhotep, there is nothing in men (or among Men) but the name of Good, the thing itself is not, for it is impossible; for a material Body receives (or Comprehends), is not as being on every side encompassed and coerced with evilness, and labors, and grieves, and desires, and wrath, and deceits, and foolish opinions.

18. And in that which is the worst of all, Imhotep, every one of the forenamed things, is here believed to be the greatest good, especially that supreme mischief the pleasures of the Belly, and the ring-leader of all evils; Error is here the absence of the Good.

19. And I give thanks to Amen, that concerning the knowledge of Good, put this assurance in my mind, that it is impossible it should be in the World.

20. For the World is the fullness of evilness; but Amen is the fullness of Good, or Good of Amen.

21. For the eminencies of all appearing Beauty, are in the Essence more pure, more sincere, and perhaps they are also the Essence of it.

22. For we must be bold to say, Imhotep, that the Essence of Amen, if He have an Essence, is that which is fair or beautiful; but no good is comprehended in this World.

23. For all things that are subject to the eye, are Idols, and as it were shadows; but those things that are not subject to the eye, are ever, especially the Essence of the Fair and the Good.

24. And as the eye cannot see Amen, so can neither the Fair, nor the Good.

25. For these are the parts of Amen that partake the Nature of the whole, proper, and familiar to Him alone, inseparable, most lovely, of which either Amen is enamored, or they are enamored of Amen.

26. If you can understand Amen, you will understand the Fair, and the Good which is most shining, and enlightening, and most enlightened by Amen.

27. For that Beauty is above comparison, and that Good is inimitable, as Amen Himself.

28. As therefore you understand Amen, you also understand the Fair and the Good, for these are incommunicable to any other living Creatures because they are inseparable from Amen.

29. If you seek Amen, you seek or long also of the Fair, for there is one way that leads to the same thing, that is Piety with Knowledge.

30. This is why, they that are ignorant, and go not in the way of Piety, dare call Man Fair and Good, never seeing so much as in a dream, what Good is; but being enfolded and wrapped up in all evil, and believing that the evil is the Good, they by that means, both use it insatiably, and are afraid to be deprived of it; and therefore they strive by all possible means, that they may not only have it, but also increase it.

31. Such, O Imhotep, are the Good and Fair things of men, which we can neither love nor hate, for this is the hardest thing of all, that we have need of them, and cannot, live without them.

## The Seventh Book. "His Secret Sermon On The Mount."

**1. Imhotep: "In the general Speeches, O Father, discoursing the Divinity, you speak enigmatically, and did not clearly reveal yourself, saying, that no man can be saved before Regeneration.**

2. And when I did humbly beg you, at the going up the Mountain after you had discoursed to me, having a great desire, to learn this Argument of Regeneration; because among all the rest, I am ignorant only of this you told me you would impart it to me, when I would estrange myself from the World; After which I made myself ready, and have vindicated the understanding that is in me, from the deceit of the World.

3. Now then fulfill my defects, and as you said instruct me of Regeneration, either by word of mouth or secretly; for I do not know, O Tehuti, of what Substance, or what Womb or what Seed a Man is born."

4. Tehuti: "O Son, this Wisdom is to be understood in silence, and the Seed is the true Good."

5. Imhotep: "Who sows it, O Father? For I am utterly ignorant and doubtful."

6. Tehuti: "The Will of Amen, O Son."

7. "And what manner of Man is he that is born so? For in this point, I am clean deprived of the Essence that understands in me."

8. Tehuti: "The Son of Amen will be another, Amen made the universe that in everything consist of all powers."

9. Imhotep: "You tell me a Riddle, Father, and do not speak as a Father to his Son."

10. Tehuti: "Son, things of this kind are not taught, but are by Amen, when he pleases, brought to remembrance."

41

11. Imhotep: "You speak of things strained, or farfetched, and impossible, Father; and therefore I will directly contradict them."

12. Tehuti: "Do you want to prove a stranger, Son, to your Father's kind?"

13. "Do not envy me, Father, or pardon me, I am your Natural Son; discourse to me the manner of Regeneration."

14. Tehuti: "What shall I say, O my Son? I have nothing to say more than this, that I see in myself an unfeigned sight or spectacle, made by the mercy of Amen, and I am gone out of myself into an immortal body, and am riot now what I was before, but was begotten in Mind.

15.This thing is not taught, nor is it to be seen in this formed Element; for which the first compound form was neglected by me; and that I am now separated from it; for I have both the touch and the measure of it, yet am I now estranged from them.

16. You see, O Son, with your eyes; but though you look never so steadfastly at me, with the Body, and bodily sight, you cannot see, nor understand what I am now."

17. Imhotep: "You have driven me, O Father, into no small fury and distraction of mind, for I do not now see myself."

18. Tehuti: "I wish, O Son, that you also were gone out of yourself, like them that dream in their sleep."

19. Imhotep: "Then tell me this, who is the Author and Maker of Regeneration?"

20. Tehuti: "The child of Amen, one Man by the Will of Amen."

21. Imhotep: "Now, O Father, you have put me to silence for ever and all my former thoughts have quite left and forsaken me, for I see the greatness, and shape of all things here below, and nothing but falsehood in them all.

22. And since this mortal Form is daily changed, and turned by this time into increase, and diminution, as being falsehood; what therefore is true, O Tehuti?"

23. Tehuti: "That, O Son, which is not troubled, nor bounded; not colored, not figured, not changed; that which is naked, bright, comprehensible only of itself, unalterable, divine."

24. Imhotep: "Now I am mad, indeed, Father; for when I thought me to have been made a wise man by you, with these thoughts you have dulled all my senses."

25. Tehuti: "Yet is it so, as I say, O Son, He that Looks Only upon that which is carried upward as Fire, that which is carried downward as Earth, that which is moist as Water, and that which blows or is subject to blast as Air; how can he sensibly understand that which is neither hard, nor moist, nor tangible, nor perspicuous, seeing it is only understood in power and operation; but I appeal to and pray to the Mind which alone can understand the Generation, which is in Amen."

26. Imhotep: "Then am I, O Father, utterly unable to do it?"

27. Tehuti: "Amen forbid, Son, rather draw or pull Him to you (or Study to Know Him) and He will come, be Willing, and it will be done; quiet (or make idle) the Senses of the Body, purging yourself from unreasonable brutal torments of matter."

28. Imhotep: "Have I any revengers or tormentors in myself, Father?"

29. Tehuti: "Yes, and not a few of them, but many and fearful ones."

30. Imhotep: "I do not know them, Father."

31. Tehuti: "One Torment, Son, is Ignorance. A second; Sorrow. A third; Intemperance. A fourth; Concupiscence. A fifth; Injustice. A sixth; Covetousness. A seventh; Deceit. An eighth; Envy. A ninth; Fraud or Guile. A tenth; Wrath. An eleventh; Rashness. A twelfth; Maliciousness.

32. They are in number twelve, and under these many more; some which through the prison of the body, do force the inwardly placed Man to suffer sensibly.

33. And they do not suddenly or easily depart from him that has obtained mercy of Amen; and in this consists, both the manner and the reason of Regeneration.

34. For the rest, O Son, hold your peace, and praise Amen in silence, and by that means, the mercy of Amen will not cease, or be wanting to us.

35. Therefore rejoice, my Son, from now forward, being purged by the powers of Amen, to the Knowledge of the Truth.

36. For the revelation of Amen has come to us, and when that came all Ignorance was cast out.

37. The knowledge of Joy is come to us, and when that comes, Sorrow will fly away to them that are capable of it.

38. I call to Joy, the power of Temperance, a power whose Virtue is most sweet; Let us take her to ourselves, O Son, most willingly, for at her coming has she put away Intemperance.

39. Now I call the fourth, Continence, the power which is over Concupiscence. This, O Son, is the stable and firm foundation of Justice.

40. For see, how without Labor, she has chased away injustice and we are justified, O Son, when Injustice is away.

41. The sixth Virtue which comes into us, I call Communion, which is against Covetousness.

42. And when that (Covetousness) is gone, I call Truth; and when she comes, Error and Deceit vanishes.

43. See, O Son, how the Good is fulfilled by the access of Truth; for by this

means, Envy is gone from us; for Truth is accompanied with the Good, together also with Life and Light.

44. And there came no more torments of Darkness, but being overcome, they all fled away suddenly, and tumultuously.

45. You have understood, O Son, the manner of Regeneration; for on the coming of these Ten, the Intellectual Generation is perfected, and then it drives away the twelve; and we have seen it in the Generation itself.

46. Whoever therefore has of Mercy obtained this Generation which is according to Amen, he leaving all bodily sense, knows himself to consist of divine things, and rejoice, being made by Amen stable and immutable."

47. Imhotep: "O Father, I conceive and understand, not by the sight of my eyes, but by the Intellectual Operation, which is by the Powers. I am in Heaven, in the Earth, in the Water, in the Air, I am in living Creatures, in the Plants, in the Womb, everywhere.

48. Yet tell me further, this one thing, how are the torments of Darkness, being in number twelve, driven away and expelled by the Ten powers? What is the manner of it, Tehuti?"

49. Tehuti; "This Tabernacle, O Son, consists of the Zodiacal Circle; and this consisting of twelve numbers, the Idea of one; but all formed Nature admit of divers Conjugations to the deceiving of Man.

50. And though they be different in themselves, they are united in practice (as for example, Rashness is inseparable from Anger) and they are also indeterminate. Therefore with good Reason, do they make their departure, being driven away by the Ten powers; that is to say, By the dead.

51. For the number of Ten, O Son, is the Producer of Souls. And there Life and Light are united, where the number of Unity is born of the Spirit.

52. Therefore according to Reason, Unity has the number of Ten, and the number of Ten has Unity."

53. Imhotep: "O Father, I now see the Universe, and myself in the Mind."

54. Tehuti: "This is Regeneration, O Son, that we should not any longer fix our imagination on this Body, subject to the three dimensions, according to this Speech which we have now commented, That we may not at all calumniate the Universe."

55. Imhotep: "Tell me, O Father, This Body that consists of Powers will it ever admit of any Dissolution?"

56. Tehuti: "Good words, Son, and speak not of things impossible; for doing so you will sin, and the eye of your mind will grow wicked.

57. The sensible Body of Nature is far from the Essential Generation; for that is subject to Dissolution, but this not; and that is mortal, but this immortal. Do you not know that you are born an Amen and the Son of the One, as I am."

58. Imhotep: "How willingly would I, O Father, hear that praise given by a Hymn, which you say, thou heard from the Powers when I was in the Octonary."

59. Tehuti: "As the Sesen said by way of Oracle to the Octonary, You do well, O Son, to desire the Solution of the Tabernacle, for you are purified.

60. Sesen, the Mind of absolute Power and Authority, has delivered no more to me, than those that are written; knowing that of myself, I can understand all things, and hear, and see what I will. And he commanded me to do those things that are good; and therefore all the Powers that are in me sing."

61. Imhotep: "I wish to hear you, O Father, and understand these things."

62. Tehuti: "Be quiet, O Son, and now listen to that harmonious blessing and thanksgiving; the hymn of Regeneration, which I did not determine to have spoken of so plainly, but to yourself in the end of all.

63. Why this is not taught, but hid in silence.

64. So then, O Son, do you standing in the open Air, worship looking to the North Wind, about the going down of the Sun, and to the South, when the Sun rises; and now keep silence, Son. The Secret Song. The Holy Speech.

65. Let all the Nature of the world entertain the hearing of this Hymn.

66. Be opened, O Earth, and let all the Treasure of the Rain be opened.

67. You Trees tremble not, for I will sing and praise the Lord of the Creation, and the All and the One.

68. Be opened you Heavens, your Winds stand still, and let the Immortal Circle of Amen receive these words.

69. For I will sing, and praise Him that created all things, that fixed the Earth, and hung up the Heavens, and commanded the sweet Water to come out of the Ocean; into all the World inhabited, and not inhabited, to the use and nourishment of all things, or men.

70. That commanded the fire to shine for very action, both to the Neter and Men.

71. Let us altogether give Him blessing, which rides on the Heavens, the Creator of all Nature.

72. It is He that is the Eye of the Mind, and Will accept the praise of my Powers.

71. O all you Powers that are in me, praise the One and the All.

74. Sing together with my Will, all you Powers that are in me.

75. O Holy Knowledge, being enlightened by You, I magnify the intelligible Light, and rejoice in the Joy of the Mind.

76. All my Powers sing praise with me, and You my Continence, sing praise my Righteousness by me; praise that which is righteous.

77. O Communion which is in me, praise the All.

78. By me the Truth sings praise to the Truth, the Good praises the Good.

79. O Life, O Light from us, to You comes this praise and thanksgiving.

80. I give thanks to You, O Father, the operation or act of my Powers.

81. I give thanks to You, O Amen, the power of my operations.

82. By me Your Word sings praise to You, receive by me this reasonable (or verbal) sacrifice in words.

83. The powers that are in me cry these things, they praise the All, they fulfill Your Will; Your Will and Counsel is from You to You.

84. O All, receive a reasonable Sacrifice from all things.

85. O Life, save all that is in us; O Light enlighten, O Amen the Spirit; for the Mind guides or feeds the Word; O Spirit bearing Workman.

86. You are Amen, Your Man cries these things to You through by the Fire, by the Air, by the Earth, by the Water, by the Spirit, by Your Creatures.

87. From eternity I have found (means to) bless and praise You, and I have what I seek, for I rest in Your Will."

88. Imhotep: "O Father, I see you have sung this Song of praise and blessing with your whole Will; and therefore have I put and placed it in my World."

89. Tehuti: "Say in your intelligible World, O Son."

90. Imhotep: "I do mean in my Intelligible World, for by your Hymn and Song of Praise my mind is enlightened; and gladly would I send from my Understanding a Thanksgiving to Amen."

91. Tehuti: "Not rashly, O Son."

92. Imhotep: "In my mind, O Father."

93. Tehuti: "Those things that I see and contemplate, I infuse into you; and therefore say, Your son Imhotep, the Author of Your succeeding Generations, I send to Amen these reasonable Sacrifices.

94. O Amen, You are the Father, You are the Lord, You are the Mind, accept these reasonable Sacrifices which You require of me.

95. For all things are done as the Mind wills.

96. You, O Son, send this acceptable Sacrifice to Amen, the Father of all things; but propound it also, O Son, by Word."

97. Imhotep: "I thank you, Father, you have advised and instructed me as to give praise and thanks."

98. Tehuti: "I am glad, O Son, to see the Truth bring forth the Fruits of Good things, and such immortal branches.

99. And learn this from me: Above all other virtues entertain Silence, and impart to no man, O Son, the tradition of Regeneration, lest we be reputed Calumniators; For we both have now sufficiently meditated, I in speaking, you in hearing. And now you intellectually know yourself and our Father.

## The Eighth Book. "That The Greatest Evil In Man, Is The Not Knowing Amen."

1. Where are you carried, O Men, drunken with drinking up the strong Wine of Ignorance? Which seeing you cannot bear: Why do you not vomit it up again?

2. Stand, and be sober, and look up again with the eyes of your heart; and if you cannot all do so, yet do as many as you can.

3. For the malice of Ignorance surrendered all the Earth, and corrupted the Soul, shut up in the Body not suffering it to arrive at the Havens of Salvation.

4. Suffer not yourselves to be carried with the great stream, but stem the tide, you that can lay hold of the Haven of Safety, and make your full course towards it.

5. Seek one that may lead you by the hand, and conduct you to the door of Truth and Knowledge, where the clear Light is that is pure from Darkness, where there is not one drunken, but all are sober and in their heart look up to Him, whose pleasure it is to be seen.

6. For He cannot be heard with ears, nor seen with eyes, nor expressed in words; but only in mind and heart.

7. But first you must tear to pieces and break through the garment you wear; the web of Ignorance, the foundation of all Mischief; the bond of Corruption; the dark Covertures; the living Death; the sensible carcass, the tomb, carried about with us; the domestic thief which in what he loves us, hates us, envies us.

8. Such is the hurtful Apparel, with which you are clothed, which draws and pulls you downward by its own self; lest looking up, and seeing the beauty of Truth, and the Good that is reposed in it, you should hate the wickedness of this garment, and understand the traps and ambushes, which it has laid for you.

9. Therefore does it Labor to make good those things that seem and are by the Senses, judged and determined; and the things that are truly, it hides, and envelopes in such matter, filling what it presents to you, with hateful pleasure, that you can neither hear what you should hear, nor see what you should see.

## The Ninth Book. "A Universal Sermon To Imhotep."

1. Tehuti: "All that is moved, O Imhotep, is it not moved in some thing, and by some thing?"

2. Imhotep: "Yes, indeed."

3. Tehuti: "Must not that, in which a thing is moved, of necessity be greater than the thing that is moved?"

4. Imhotep: "Of necessity."

5. Tehuti: "And that which moves, is it not stronger than that which is moved?"

6. Imhotep: "It is stronger."

7. Tehuti: "That in which a thing is moved, must it not need to have a Nature, contrary to that of the thing that is moved?"

8. Imhotep: "It must."

9. Tehuti: "Is not this great World a Body, than, which there is no greater?"

10. Imhotep: "Yes, confessedly."

11. Tehuti: "And is it not solid, as filled with many great bodies, and indeed, with all the Bodies that are?"

12. Imhotep: "It is so."

13. Tehuti: "And is it not the World a Body, and a Body that is moved?"

14. Imhotep: "It is."

15. Tehuti: "Then what kind of a place must it be, in which it is moved, and of what Nature? Must it not be much bigger, that it may receive the continuity of Motion? And lest that which is moved should for want of room, he stayed, and hindered in the Motion?"

16. Imhotep: "It must need to be an immense thing, Tehuti, but of what Nature?"

17. Tehuti: "Of a contrary Nature, O Imhotep, but is not the Nature of things divine, contrary to a Body?"

18. Imhotep: "Confessedly."

19. Tehuti: "Therefore the place is Divine; but that which is Divine, is either some Divine thing or Amen Himself and by something Divine, I do not mean that which was made or produced.

20. If therefore it be Divine, it is an Essence or Substance but if it be Amen, it is above Essence; but He is otherwise intelligible.

21. For the first, Amen is intelligible, not to Himself, but to us, for that which is intelligible, is subject to that which understands by Sense.

22. Therefore Amen is not intelligible to Himself, for not being any other thing from that which is understood, He cannot be understood by Himself.

23. But He is another thing from us, and therefore He is understood by us.

24. If therefore Place be intelligible, it is not Place but Amen, but if Amen be intelligible, He is intelligible not as Place, but as a capable Operation.

25. Now everything that is moved is moved, not in or by that which is moved, but in that which stand or rest, and that which moves stands or rest, for it is impossible it should be moved with it."

26. Imhotep: "How then, O Tehuti, are those things that are here moved with the things that are Moved? For you say that the Spheres that wander are moved by the Sphere that wanders not."

27. Tehuti: "That, O Imhotep, is not a moving together, but a countermotion, for they are not moved after the same manner, but contrary one to the other; and contrariety has a standing resistance of motion for resistance is a staying of motion.

53

28. Therefore the wandering Spheres being moved contrarily to that Sphere, which wanders not, will have one from another contrariety standing of itself.

29. For this Bear which you see neither rise nor go down, but turning always about the same; dost thou think it moves or stands still?"

30. Imhotep: "I think it moves, Tehuti."

31. Tehuti: "What motion, O Imhotep?"

32. Imhotep: "A motion that is always carried about the same."

33. "But the Circulation which is about the same, and the motion about the same, are both hidden; for that which is about the same forbids that which is above the same, if it stands to that which is about the same.

34. And so the contrary motion stands fast always, being always established by the contrariety.

35. But I will give you concerning this matter, an earthly example that may be seen with eyes.

36. Look at any of these living Creatures on Earth, as Man for example, and see him swimming; for as the Water is carried one way, the reluctance or resistance of his feet and hands is made a stabilizer to the man, that he should not be carried with the Water, nor sink underneath it."

37. Imhotep: "You have laid down a very clear example, Tehuti."

38. Tehuti: "Therefore every motion is in stability, and is moved of stability.

39. The motion then of the World, and of every material living thing, happens not to be done by those things that are without the World, but by those things within it, a Soul, or Spirit, or some other Divine thing, to those things which are without it.

40. For an inanimate Body, does not now, much less a Body if it be fully inanimate."

41. Imhotep: "What do you mean by this, O Tehuti, Wood and Stones, and all other inanimate things, are they not moving Bodies?"

42. Tehuti: "By no means, O Imhotep, for that within the Body which moves the inanimate thing, is not the Body, that moves both as well the Body of that which bears, as the Body of that which is born; for one dead or inanimate thing, cannot move another; that which moves, must need to be alive for it to move.

43. You see, therefore how the Soul is surcharged, when it carries two Bodies.

44. And now it is manifest, that the things that are moved are moved in something, and by something."

45 Imhotep: "The things that are, O Tehuti, must need to be moved in that which is void or empty, Vacuum."

46. "Be advised, O Imhotep, for of all the things that are, there is nothing empty, only that which is not, is empty and a stranger to existence or being.

47. But that which is, could not be if it were not full of existence, for that which is in being or existence can never be made empty."

48. Imhotep: "Are there not therefore some things that are empty, O Tehuti, as an empty Barrel, an empty shed, an empty Well, an empty Wine-Press, and many such like?"

49. Tehuti: "O the grossness of your Error, O Imhotep, those things that are most full and replenished, do you account them void and empty."

50. Imhotep: "What do you mean, Tehuti?"

51. Tehuti: "Is not the Air a Body?"

52. Imhotep: "It is a Body."

53. Tehuti: "Why then does this Body not pass through all things that are and passing through them, fill them? And does that Body not consist of the mixture of the four? Therefore all those you call empty are full of Air.

54. Therefore those things that you call empty, you should call them hollow, not empty, for they exist and are full of Air and Spirit."

55. Imhotep: "This reason is beyond all contradiction, O Tehuti, but what will we call the Place in which the whole Universe is moved?"

56. Tehuti: "Call it immaterial, O Imhotep."

57. Imhotep: "What is that immaterial or Divine?"

58. Tehuti: "The Mind and Reason, the whole, fully comprehending itself, free from all Body, undeceivable, invisible, impassible from a Body itself, standing fast in itself, capable of all things, and that favor of the things that are.

59. Of which the Good, the Truth, the Archetypal Light, the Archetype of the Soul, are as it were Beams."

60. Imhotep: "Why then, what is Amen?"

61. Tehuti: "That which is none of these things, yet is, and is the cause of Being to all; and every one of the things that are; for He left nothing destitute of Being.

62. And all things are made of things that are, and not of things that are not; for the things that are not, have not the nature to be able to be made; and again, the things that are, have not the nature never to be, or not to be at all."

63. Imhotep: "What do you then say at length, that Amen is?"

64. Tehuti: "Amen is not a Mind, but the Cause that the Mind is; not a Spirit, but the Cause that the Spirit is; not Light, but the Cause that Light is.

65. Therefore we must worship Amen by these two Appellations which are proper to Him alone, and to no other.

66. For neither of all the other, which are called Neter, nor of Men, nor Spirits, or Angels, can anyone be, though never so little, good, save only Amen alone.

67. And this He is, and nothing else; but all other things are separable from the nature of Good.

68. For the Body and the Soul have no place that is capable of or can contain the Good.

69. For the greatness of Good, is as great as the Existence of all things, that are both bodily and Divine, both sensible and intelligible.

70. This is the Good, even Amen.

71. See therefore that you do not at any time, call ought else Good, for so you will be impious, or any else Amen, but only the Good, for so you will again be impious.

72. In Word it is often said by all men the Good, but all men do not understand what it is; but through Ignorance they call both the Neter, and some men Good, that can never either be or be made so.

73. Therefore all the other Neter are honored with the title and appellation of Amen, but Amen is the Good, not according to Heaven, but Nature.

74. For there is one Nature of Amen, even the Good, and one kind of them both, from where are all kinds.

75. For he that is Good, is the giver of all things, and takes nothing and therefore Amen gives all things and receives nothing.

76. The other title and appellation, is the Father, because of his making all things; for it is the part of a Father to make.

77. Therefore it has been the greatest and most Religious care in this life, to them that are wise, and well-minded, to produce children.

78. As likewise it is the greatest misfortune and impiety for any to be separated from men, without children; and this man is punished after death by the Spirits, and the punishment is this, To have the Soul of this childless man, adjudged and condemned to a Body, that neither has the nature of a man, nor of a woman, which is an accursed thing under the Sun.

79. Therefore, O Imhotep, never congratulate any man that is childless; but on the contrary, pity his misfortune, knowing what punishment abides, and is prepared for him.

80. Let so many, and such manner of things, O Imhotep, be said as a certain precognition of all things in Nature."

## The Tenth Book. "The Mind to Tehuti."

1. Refrain your speech, O Tehuti, and call to mind those things that are said: but I will not delay to speak what comes into my mind, since many men have spoken many things, and those very different, concerning the Universe and Good; but I have not learned the Truth.

2. Therefore, the Lord makes it plain to me in this point; for I will believe You only, for the manifestation of these things.

3. Then said the Mind how the case stands.

4. Amen and all.

5. Amen, Eternity, the World, Time, Generation.

6. Amen made Eternity, Eternity the World; the World Time, and Time Generation.

7. Of Amen, as it were the Substance, is the Good, the Fair, Blessedness, Wisdom.

8. Of Eternity, Identity, or Selfness.

9. Of the World, Order.

10. Of Time, Change.

11. Of Generation, Life, and Death.

12. But the Operation of Amen, is Mind and Soul.

13. Of Eternity, Permanence, or Long-lasting, and Immortality.

14. Of the World, Restitution, and Decay or Destruction.

15. Of Time, Augmentation and Diminution.

16. And of Generation, Qualities.

17. Therefore Eternity is in Amen.

18. The World in Eternity.

19. Time in the World.

20. And Generation in Time.

21. And Eternity stands about Amen.

22. The World is moved in Eternity.

23. Time is determined in the World.

24. Generation is done in Time.

25. Therefore the Spring and Fountain of all things is Amen.

26. The Substance Eternity.

27. The Matter is the World.

28. The Power of Amen is Eternity.

29. And the Work of Eternity is the World not yet made, and yet ever made by Eternity.

30. Therefore will nothing be destroyed at any time, for Eternity is incorruptible.

31. Neither can anything perish, or be destroyed in the World, the World being contained and embraced by eternity.

32. But what is the Wisdom of Amen? Even the Good, and the Fair and Blessedness, and every Virtue, and Eternity.

33. Eternity therefore put into the Matter Immortality and Everlastingness; for the Generation of that depends upon Eternity, even as Eternity does of Amen.

34. For Generation and Time, in Heaven, and in Earth, are of a double Nature; in Heaven they are unchangeable and incorruptible, but on Earth they are changeable and corruptible.

35. And the Soul of Eternity is Amen; and the Soul of the World Eternity; and of the Earth, Heaven.

36. Amen is in the Mind, the Mind in the Soul, the Soul in the Matter, all things by Eternity.

37. All this Universal Body, in which are all Bodies, is full of Soul, the Soul full of Mind, the Mind full of Amen.

38. For within He fills them, and without He contains them, quickening the Universe.

39. Without He quickens this perfect living thing the World, and within all living Creatures.

40. And above in Heaven He abides in Identity or Selfness, but below on Earth He changes Generation.

41. Eternity comprehends the World, either by Necessity, or Providence, or Nature.

42. And if any man will think any other thing, it is Amen that actuates, or operates this All.

43. But the operation or Act of Amen, is power insuperable, to which none may compare anything, either Human or Divine.

44. Therefore, O Tehuti, think none of these things below, or the things above, in any wise like to Amen, for if you do you error from the Truth.

45. For nothing can be like the unlike, and only and One; nor may you think that He has given of His Power to any other thing.

46. For who after Him can make anything, either of Life, or Immortality; of Change or of Quality and Himself what other thing should He make?

47. For Amen is not idle, for then all things would be idle; for all things are full of Amen.

48. But there is not anywhere in the world such a thing as Idleness; for Idleness is a name that implies a thing void or empty, both of a Doer and a thing done.

49. But all things must necessarily be made or done both always and according to the nature of every place.

50. For he that makes or does is in all things, yet not fastened or comprehended in anything, nor making or doing one thing, but all things.

51. For being an active or operating Power and sufficient of Himself for the things that are made, and the things that are made are under Him.

52. Look at, through me, the World is subject to your sight, and understand exactly the Beauty of it.

53. A Body everlasting, than which, there is nothing more ancient, yet always vigorous and young.

54. See also the seven Worlds set over us, adorned with an everlasting Order, and filling Eternity, with a different course.

55. For all things are full of Light, but the Fire is nowhere.

56. For the friendship and commixture of contraries and unlike became Light

shining from the Act or Operation of Amen, the Father of all Good, the Prince of all Order, and the Ruler of the seven Worlds.

57. Look also upon the Moon, the forerunner of them all, the Instrument of Nature, and which changes the Matter here below.

58. Behold the Earth, the middle of the whole, the firm and stable Foundation of the Fair World, the Feeder and Nurse of Earthly things.

59. Consider moreover, how great the multitude is of immortal living things, and of mortal ones also; and see the Moon going about in the midst of both, to wit, of things immortal and mortal.

60. But all things are full of Soul, and all things are properly moved by it; some things about the Heaven, and some things about the Earth, and neither of those on the right hand to the left; nor those on the left hand to the right; nor those things that are above, downward; nor those things that are below, upwards.

61. And that all these things are made, O beloved Tehuti, you do not need to learn from me.

62. For they are Bodies, and have a Soul, and are moved.

63. And that all these should come together into one, it is impossible without something, to gather them together.

64. Therefore there must be some such ones and He altogether one.

65. For seeing that the motions are divers, and many, and the Bodies not for one order is not kept by many alike, and yet one ordered swiftness among them all; It is impossible there should be two or more Makers.

66. But in the weaker, there would be jealousy of the stronger and therefor also Contentions.

67. And if there were one Maker of mutable and mortal living creatures, he

would desire also to make immortal ones, as he that were the Maker of immortal ones, would do to make mortal.

68. Moreover also, if there were two, the Matter being one, who should be chief, or have the disposing of the facture?

69. Or if both of them, which of them the greater part?

70. But think so that every living Body has its consistence of Matter and Soul; and of that which is immortal, and that which is mortal, and unreasonable.

71. For all living Bodies have a Soul; and those things that are not living are only matter by itself.

72. And the Soul likewise of itself drawing near her Maker, is the Cause of Life and Being and Being the cause of Life, is after a manner, the cause of immortal things.

73. How then are mortal creatures, other from immortal?

74. Or how cannot He make living creatures that causes immortal things and immortality?

75. That there is some Body that does these things it is apparent, and that He is also one, it is most manifest.

76. For there is one Soul, one Life and one Matter.

77. Who is this? Who can it be? Other than the One Amen.

78. For whom else can it benefit, to make living things, save only Amen alone?

79. There is therefore one Amen.

80. For it is a ridiculous thing to confess the World to be one Sun, one Moon,

one Divinity; and yet to have I know not how many Neter.

81. He therefore being One, does all things in many things.

82. And what great thing is it for Amen to make Life and Soul, and Immortality, and Change, when you yourself do so many things?

83. For you both sees, speaks and hears, smells, tastes and touches, walks, understands, and breathes.

84. And it is not one that sees, and another that hears, and another that speaks, and another that touches, and another that smells, and another that walks, and another that understand, and another that breathes, but One that does all these things.

85. Yet neither can these things possibly be without Amen.

86. For as you, if you should cease from doing these things, were not a living creature; so if Amen should cease from those, He were not (which is not lawful to say) any longer Amen.

87. For if it be already energized, that nothing can be idle or empty, how much more may be affirmed of Amen?

88. For if there be any thing which He does not do, then is He (if it were lawful to say so) imperfect.

89. Whereas feeling He is not idle, but perfect, certainly He does all things.

90. Now give yourself to me, O Tehuti, for a little while you will more easily understand, that it is the necessary work of Amen that all things should be made or done that are done or were once done, or will be done.

91. And this, O best Beloved, is life.

92. And this is the Fair.

93. And this is the Good.

94. And this is Amen.

95. And if you want to understand this by work also, mark what happens to yourself, when you want to generate.

96. And yet this is not like to Him; for He is not sensible of pleasure, for neither has He any other.

97. But being Himself the only Workman He is always in the Work, Himself being that which He does or makes.

98. For all things, if they were separated from Him, must need to fall and die, as there being no life in them.

99. And again, if all things be living creatures, both which are in Heaven, and on Earth; and that there be one Life in all things which are made by Amen, and that is Amen, then certainly all things are made, or done by Amen.

100. Life is the union of the Mind and the Soul.

101. But death is not the destruction of those things that were gathered together, but a dissolving of the Union.

102. The Image therefore of Amen is Eternity, of Eternity the Sun, of the Sun the World, of the World, Man.

103. But the people say, That changing is Death, because the Body is dissolved, and the Life goes into that which appears not.

104. By this discourse, my dearest Tehuti, I affirm as you hear, That the World is changed, because every day part of it becomes invisible; but that it is never dissolved.

105. And these are the Passions of the World, Revolutions and Change, and Revolution is a turning, but Change is Renovation.

106. And the World being all formed, hath not the forms lying without it, but itself changes in itself.

107. Seeing then the World is all formed, what must He be that made it? For without form He cannot be.

108. And if He be all formed, He will be kept like the World, but if He has but one form, He will be in this regard less than the World.

109. What do we then say that He is? We will not raise any doubts by our speech; for nothing that is doubtful concerning Amen, is yet known.

110. He has therefore one Idea which is proper to Him, which because it is Divine is not subject to the sight, and yet shows all forms by the Bodies.

111. And do not wonder, if there be an incorruptible Idea.

112. For they are like the Margents of that Speech which is in writing; for they seem to be high and swelling, but they are by nature smooth and even.

113. But understand well this that I say, more boldly, for it is more true; As a man cannot live without life, so neither can Amen live, not doing good.

114. For this is, as it were, the Life and Motion of Amen, to move all things, and quicken them.

115. But some of the things I have said, must have a particular explication; Understand then what I say.

116. All things are in Amen, not as lying in a place; for Place is both a Body, and unmovable, and those things that are there placed, have no motion.

117. For they lie otherwise in that which is Divine, than in the fantasy or to appearance.

118. Consider him that contains all things, and understand, that nothing is more capacious, than that which is immaterial, nothing swifter, and nothing

more powerful, but it is most capacious, most swift and most strong.

119. And judge of this by yourself, command your Soul to go into India, and sooner than you can command it, it will be there.

120. Command it likewise to pass over the Ocean, and suddenly it will be there; Not as passing from place to place, but suddenly it will be there.

121. Command it to fly into Heaven, and it will need no Wings, neither will anything hinder it; not the fire of the Sun, not the Ether, not the turning of the Spheres, not the bodies of any of the other Stars, but cutting through all, it will fly up to the last, and furthest Body.

122. And if you want to even break the whole, and see those things that are without the World (if there be any thing without) you may.

123. Look at how great power, how great swiftness you have! Can you do all these things, and cannot Amen?

124. After this manner therefore contemplate Amen to have the entire whole World to Himself, as it were all thoughts, or intellections.

125. If therefore you want to not equal yourself to Amen, you cannot understand Amen.

126. For the like is intelligible by the like.

127. Increase yourself into an immeasurable greatness, leaping beyond every Body; and transcending all Time, become Eternity and you will understand Amen: If you believe in yourself that nothing is impossible, but accounts yourself immortal, and that you can understand all things, every Art, every Science and the manner and custom of every living thing.

128. Become higher than all height, lower than all depths, comprehend in yourself, the qualities of all the Creatures, of the Fire, the Water, the Dry and Moist; and conceive likewise, that you can at once be everywhere in the Sea, in the Earth.

129. You will at once understand yourself, not yet produced in the Womb, young, old, to be dead, the things after death, and all these together as also times, places, deeds, qualities, quantities, or else you cannot yet understand Amen.

130. But if you shut up your Soul in the Body and abuse it, and say, I understand nothing, I can do nothing, I am afraid of the Sea, I cannot climb up into Heaven, I know not who I am, I cannot tell what I will be; what have you to do with Amen; for you can understand none of those Fair and Good things; be a lover of the Body and Evil.

131. For it is the greatest evil, not to know Amen.

132. But to be able to know and to will, and to hope, is the straight way, and Divine way, proper to the Good; and it will everywhere meet you, and everywhere be seen by you, plain and easy, when you do not expect or look for it; it will meet you, waking, sleeping, sailing, traveling, by night, by day, when you speak, and when you keep silence.

133. For there is nothing which is not the Image of Amen.

134. And yet you say, Amen is invisible, but be advised, for who is more manifest than He.

135. For therefore has He made all things, that you by all things may see Him.

136. This is the Good of Amen; this is His Virtue, to appear, and to be seen in all things.

137. There is nothing invisible, no, not of those things that are immaterial.

138. The Mind is seen in Understanding, and Amen is seen in doing or making.

139. Let these things so far forth, be made manifest to you, O Tehuti.

140. Understand in like manner, all other things by yourself, and you will not be deceived.

## The Eleventh Book. "Of the Common Mind to Imhotep. "

1. "The Mind, O Imhotep, is of the very Essence of Amen, if yet there be any Essence of Amen.

2. What kind of Essence that is, He alone knows Himself exactly.

3. The Mind therefore is not cut off, or divided from the essentiality of Amen, but united as the light of the sun.

4. And this mind in men, is Amen, and therefore are some men Divine, and their Humanity is near Divinity.

5. For the good Spirit called the Neter immortal men, and men mortal Neter.

6. But in the brutal Beasts, or unreasonable living creatures, the Mind is their Nature.

7. For where there is a Soul, there is the Mind, as where there is Life, there is also a Soul.

8. In living Creatures therefore, that are without Reason, the Soul is Life, void of the operations of the Mind.

9. For the Mind is the Benefactor of the Souls of men, and works to the proper Good.

10. And in unreasonable things it co-operates with the Nature of every one of them, but in men it works against their Natures.

11. For the Soul being in the Body, is straightaway made Evil by Sorrow, and Grief and Pleasure or Delight.

12. For Grief and Pleasure flow like Juices from the compound Body, where to, when the Soul entreats, or descends, she is moistened and tainted with them.

13. As many Souls therefore, as the Mind governs or overrules, to them it shows its own Light, resisting their prepossessions or presumptions.

14. As a good Physician grieves the Body, prepossessed of a disease, by burning or lancing it for health's sake.

15. After the same manner also, the Mind grieves the Soul, by drawing it out of Pleasure, from where every disease of the Soul proceed.

16. But the great Disease of the Soul is Atheism because that opinion follows to all Evil and no Good.

17. Therefore the Mind resisting it procures Good to the Soul, as a Physician health to the Body.

18. But as many Souls of Men, as do not admit or entertain the Mind for their Governor, do suffer the same thing that the Soul of unreasonable living things.

19. For the Soul being a Co-operator with them, permits or leaves them to their desires, whereto they are carried by the torrent of their Appetite, and so tend to brutality.

20. And as Brutal Beasts, they are angry without reason, and they desire without reason, and never cease, nor are satisfied with evil.

21. For unreasonable Angers and Desires, are the most exceeding Evils.

22. And therefore has Amen set the Mind over these, as a Revenge and Reprove of them."

23. Imhotep: "Here, O Father, that discourse of Fate or Destiny which you made to me, is in danger to be overthrown; for if it be fatal for any man to commit Adultery or Sacrilege or do any evil, he is punished also, though he of necessity do the work of Fate or Destiny."

24. Tehuti: "All things, O Son, are the work of Fate, and without it, can no

bodily thing, either Good or Evil, be done.

25. For it is decreed by Fate, that he that cloth any evil, should also suffer for it.

26. And therefore he cloth it, that he may suffer that which he suffers, because he did it.

27. But for the present let alone that speech, concerning Evil and Fate, for at other times we have spoken of it.

28. Now our discourse is about the Mind, and what it can do, and how it differs, and is in men such a one, but in brutal Beasts changed.

29. And again, in Brutal Beasts it is not beneficial, but in men by quenching both their Anger and Selfish desire.

30. And of men you must understand some to be rational or governed by reason, and some irrational.

31. But all men are subject to Fate, and to Generation, and Changes, for these are the beginning and end of Fate or Destiny.

32. And all men suffer those things that are decreed by Fate.

33. But rational men, over whom as we said, the Mind bears rule, do not suffer like other men, but being free from viciousness, and being not evil, they do suffer evil."

34. Imhotep: "How do you say this again, Father? An Adulterer, is he not evil? A Murderer, is he not evil? And so all others?"

35. Tehuti: "But the rational man, O Son, will not suffer for Adultery, but as the Adulterer, nor for Murder, but as the Murderer.

36.     And it is impossible to escape the Quality of Change, as of Generation, but the Viciousness, he that has the Mind, may escape.

37. And therefore, O Son, I have always heard the good Spirit say, and if He had delivered it in writing, He had much profited all mankind: For he alone, O Son, as the first born, Amen, seeing all things, truly spoke Divine words. I have heard Him say sometimes, That all Things are one thing, Especially Intelligible Bodies, or that all Especially Intelligible Bodies are one.

38. We live in Power, in Act and in Eternity.

39. Therefore a good Mind, is that which the Soul of Him is.

40. And if this be so, then no intelligible thing differs from intelligible things.

41. As therefore it is possible, that the Mind, the Prince of all things; so likewise, that the Soul that is of Amen, can do whatever it will.

42. But understand well, for this Discourse I have made to the question which you asked of me before, I mean concerning Fate and the Mind.

43. First, if, O Son, you will diligently withdraw yourself from all Contentious speeches, you will find that in Truth, the Mind, the Soul of Amen bears rule over all things, both over Fate and Law and all other things.

44. And nothing is impossible to Him, no not of the things that are of Fate.

45. Therefore, though the Soul of man be above it, let it not neglect the things that happen to be under Fate.

46. And these so far, were the excellent sayings of the good Spirit."

47. Imhotep: "Most divinely spoken, O Father, and truly and profitably, yet clear this one thing up for me.

48. You say, that in brutal Beasts the Mind works or acts after the manner of Nature, co-operating also with their (impetuous) inclinations.

49. Now the impetuous inclinations of brutal Beasts, as I conceive, are Passions. If therefore the Mind do co-operate with these impetuous

73

Inclinations, and that they are the Passions in brutal Beasts, certainly the Mind is also a Passion, conforming itself to Passions."

50. Tehuti: "Well done, Son, you ask nobly, and yet it is just that I should answer you.

51. All immaterial things, O Son, that are in the Body, are possible, no, they are properly Passions.

52. Everything that moves is immaterial; everything that is moved is a Body, and it is moved into the Bodies by the Mind. Now motion is Passion, and there they both suffer; as well that which moves, as that which is moved, as well that which rules, as that which is ruled.

53. But being freed from the Body, it is freed likewise from Passion.

54. But especially, O Son, there is nothing impassible, but all things are passable.

55. But Passion differs from that which is passable, for that (Passion) act but this suffers.

56. Bodies also of themselves do act, for either they are unmovable, or else are moved, and which so ever it be, it is a Passion.

57. But immaterial things do always act, or work, and therefore they are passable.

58. Let not therefore the appellations or names trouble you, for Action and Passion are the same thing, but that it is not grievous to use the more honorable name."

59. Imhotep: "O Father, you have delivered this Discourse most plainly."

60. Tehuti: "Consider this also, O Son, That Amen has freely bestowed on man, above all other living things, these two, to wit, Mind and Speech, or Reason, equal to immortality.

61. These if any man use, or employ on what he ought, he will differ nothing from the Immortals.

62. Yea, rather going out of the Body, he will be guided and led by them, both into the Choir and Society of the Neter, and blessed Ones."

63. Imhotep: "Do not other living Creatures use Speech, O Father?"

64. Tehuti: "No, Son, only Voice; now Speech and Voice do differ exceeding much; for Speech is common to all men, but Voice is proper to every kind of living thing."

65. Imhotep: "Yea, but the Speech of men is different. O Father, every man according to his Nation."

66. Tehuti: "It is true, O Son, they do differ: Yet as man is one so is Speech one also; and it is interpreted and found the same, both in Egypt, Persia, and Greece.

67. But you seem to me, Son, to be ignorant of the Virtue or Power, and Greatness of Speech.

68. For the blessed Amen, the good Spirit said or commanded the Soul to be in the Body, the Mind, in the Soul, the Word, or Speech, or Reason in the Mind, and the Mind in Amen, and that Amen is the Father of them all.

69. Therefore the Word is the Image of the Mind, and the Mind of Amen, and the Body of the Idea, and the Idea of the Soul.

70. Therefore of the Matter, the subtlest or smallest part is Air, of the Air the Soul, of the Soul the Mind, of the Mind Amen.

71. And Amen is about all things, and through all things, but the Mind about the Soul, the Soul about the Air, and the Air about the Matter.

72. But Necessity, and Providence, and Nature, are the Organs or Instruments of the World, and of the Order of Matter.

73. For of those things that are intelligible, everyone is but the Essence of them in Identity.

74. But of the Bodies of the whole, or universe, everyone is many things.

75. For the Bodies that are put together, and that have, and make their changes into other, having this Identity, do always save and preserve the incorruption of the Identity.

76. But in every one of the compound Bodies, there is a number.

77. For without number it is impossible there should be consistence or constitution, or composition, or dissolution.

78. But Unities do both produce and increase Numbers, and again being dissolved, come into themselves.

79. And the Matter is One.

80. But this whole World, the great Amen, and the Image of the Greater, and united to Him, and conserving the Order and Will of the Father, is the fullness of Life.

81. And there is nothing therein, through all the Eternity of the Revolutions, neither of the whole, nor of the parts which cloths not live.

82. For there is nothing dead, that either has been, or is, or will be in the World.

83. For the Father would have it as long as it lasts, to be a living thing; and therefore it must need Amen also.

84. How therefore, O Son, can there be in Amen, in the Image of the Universe, in the fullness of Life, any dead things?

85. For dying is corruption, and corruption is destruction.

86. How then can any part of the incorruptible be corrupted, or of Amen be destroyed?"

87. Imhotep: "Therefore, O Father, do not the living things in the World die, though they be parts of it?"

88. Tehuti: "Be wary in your Speech, O Son, and not deceived in the names of things.

89. For they do not die, O Son, but as compound Bodies they are dissolved.

90. But dissolution is not death; and they are dissolved, not that they may be destroyed, but that they may be made new."

91. Imhotep: "What then is the operation of Life? Is it not Motion?"

92. Tehuti: "And what is there in the World unmovable? Nothing at all, O Son."

93. Imhotep: "Why, could not the Earth seem unmovable to you, O Father?"

94. Tehuti: "No, but subject to many motions, though after a manner it alone be stable.

95. What a ridiculous thing it were, that the Nurse of all things should be unmovable, which bears and brings forth all things.

96. For it is impossible, that anything that brings forth, should bring forth without Motion.

97. And a ridiculous question it is, whether the fourth part of the whole, be idle: For the word immovable, or without Motion, signifies nothing else, but idleness.

98. Know generally, O Son, That whatever is in the World is moved either according to Augmentation or Diminution.

99. But that which is moved, lives also, yet it is not necessary, that a living thing should be or continue the same.

100. For while the whole World is together, it is unchangeable, O Son, but all the parts of it are changeable.

101. Yet nothing is corrupted or destroyed, and quite abolished but the names trouble men.

102. For Generation is not Life, but Sense; neither is Change Death, but Forgetfulness, or rather Renovated and lying hid. Or better so. For Generation is not a Creation of Life, but a Production of Things to Sense, and making them Manifest. Neither is Change Death, but an Renovation or Hiding of that which was.

103. These things being so, all things are Immortal, Matter, Life, Spirit, Soul, Mind, of which every living thing consisted.

104. Every living thing therefore is Immortal, because of the Mind, but especially Man, who both receives Amen, and converses with Him.

105. For with this living character alone is Amen familiar; in the night by dreams, in the day by Symbols or Signs.

106. And by all things could He foretell him of things to come, by Birds, by Fowls, by the Spirit, or Wind, and by an Oak.

107. This is why also Man professes to know things that: have been, things that are present, and things to come.

108. Consider this also, O Son, That every living Creature goes on one part of the World, Swimming things in Water, Land creatures upon the Earth, Flying Fowls in the Air.

109. But Man uses all these, the Earth, the Water, the Air, and the Fire, no, he sees and touches Heaven by his Sense.

110. But Amen is both about all things, and through all things, for He is both Act and Power.

111. And it is no hard thing, O Son, to understand Amen.

112. And if you want to also see Him, look upon the Necessity of things that appear, and the Providence of things that have been, and are done.

113. See the Matter being most full of Life, and so great as Amen moved with all Good, and Fair, both Neter, and Spirits, and Men."

114. Imhotep: "But these, O Father, are fully Acts or Operations."

115. Tehuti: "If they be therefore wholly Acts or Operations, O Son, by whom are they acted or operated, but by Amen?

116. Or are you ignorant, that as the parts of the World, are Heaven, and Earth, and Water, and Air; after the same manner the Members of Amen, are Life, and Immortality, and Eternity, and Spirit, and Necessity, and Providence, and Nature, and Soul, and Mind, and the Continuance or Perseverance of all these which is called Good.

117. And there is not anything of all that has been, and all that is, where Amen is not."

118. Imhotep: "What in the Matter, O Father?"

119. Tehuti: "The Matter, Son, what is it without Amen, that you should ascribe a proper place to it?

120. Or what could you think it to be? Chance some heap that is not actuated or operated.

121. But if it be actuated, by whom is it actuated? For we have said, that Acts or Operations, are the parts of Amen.

122. By whom are all living things quickened? And the Immortal, by whom are they immortalized? The things that are changeable, by whom are they changed?

123. Whether you speak of Matter, or Body, or Essence, know that all these are acts of Amen.

124. And that the Act of Matter is materiality, and of the Bodies corporality, and of Essence essentiality; and this is Amen the whole.

125. And in the whole, there is nothing that is not Amen.

126. This is why about Amen, there is neither Size, Place, Quality, Figure, or Time; for He is All, and the All, through all, and about all.

127. This Word, O Son, worship and adore. And the only service of Amen, is not to be evil."

## The Twelfth Book. "His Word."

1. The Workman made this Universal World, not with His Hands, but His Word.

2. Therefore think of Him as present everywhere, and being always, and making all things, and one above, that by His Will has framed the things that are.

3. For that is His Body, not tangible, nor visible, nor measurable, nor extensible, nor like any other body.

4. For it is neither Fire, nor Water, nor Air, nor Wind, but all these things are of Him, for being Good, He has dedicated that name to Himself alone.

5. But He would also adorn the Earth, but with the Ornament of a Divine Body.

6. And He sent Man an Immortal and a Mortal character.

7. And Man had more than all living Creatures, and the World, because of his Speech and Mind.

8. For Man became the spectator of the Works of Amen, and wondered, and acknowledged the Maker.

9. For He divided Speech among all men, but not Mind, and yet He envied not any, for Envy comes not thither, but is of abode here below in the Souls of men, that have not the Mind."

10. Imhotep: "But why, Father, did Amen not distribute the Mind to all men?"

11. "Because it pleased Him, O Son, to set that in the middle among all souls as a reward to strive for."

12. Imhotep: "And where has He set it?"

13. Tehuti: "Filling a large Cup or Bowl with it, He sent it down, giving also a herald or Proclaimer.

14. And He commanded him to proclaim these things to the souls of men.

15. Dip and wash yourself, you that are able, in this Cup or Bowl; you who believes; that you will return to him that sent this Cup; you who acknowledges whereto you were made.

16. As many therefore as understood the Proclamation and were baptized or dowsed into the Mind, these were made partakers of Knowledge, and became perfect men, receiving the Mind.

17. But as many as missed of the Proclamation, they received Speech, but not Mind, being ignorant whereto they were made, or by Whom.

18. But their senses are just like to brutal Beasts, and having their temper in Anger and Wrath, they do not admire the things worthy of looking on.

19. But fully addicted to the pleasures and desires of the Bodies, they believe that man was made for them.

20. But as many as partook of the gift of Amen, these, O Imhotep, in comparison of their works, are rather immortal than mortal men.

21. Comprehending all things in their Mind, which are upon the Earth, which are in Heaven, and if there be anything above Heaven.

22. And lifting up themselves so high, they see the Good, and seeing it, they account it a miserable calamity to make their abode here.

23. And despising all things bodily and Divine, they make haste to the One and Only.

24. So, O Imhotep, is the Knowledge of the Mind, the beholding of Divine

Things, and the Understanding of Amen, the Cup itself being Divine."

25. Imhotep: "And I, O Father, wish to be baptized and drenched in it."

26. Tehuti: "Except you first hate your body, O Son, you cannot love yourself; but loving yourself, you will have the Mind, and having the Mind, you will also partake the Knowledge or Science."

27. Imhotep: "How do you mean that, O Father?"

28. Tehuti: "Because it is impossible, O Son, to be knowledgeable about things Mortal and Divine.

29. For the things that are being two Bodies, and things immaterial, in which is the Mortal and the Divine, the Election or Choice of either is left to him that will choose; for no man can choose both.

30. And of which so ever the choice is made, the other being diminished or overcome, magnifies the act and operation of the other.

31. The choice of the chooser therefore is not only best for him that choose it, by deifying a man; but it also shows Piety and Faith towards Amen.

32. But the choice of the worse destroys a man, but covers nothing from Amen; like Pomp or Pageants, when they come around, cannot do anything themselves, but hinder; after the same manner also do many choose Pomp or Pageants of the World, being seduced by the pleasures of the Body.

33. These things being so, O Imhotep, that things have been and are so plenteously ministered to us from Amen; let them proceed also from us, without any scarcity or sparing.

34. For Amen is innocent or guiltless, but we are the causes of Evil, preferring them before the Good.

35. You see, O Son, how many Bodies we must go beyond, and how many choirs of Spirits, and what continuity and courses of Stars, that we may make haste to the One, and only Amen.

36. For the Good is not to be transcended; it is unbounded and infinite; to itself without beginning, but to us, seeming to have a beginning, even our knowledge of it.

37. For our knowledge is not the beginning of it, but shows us the beginning of its being known to us.

38. Let us therefore lay hold of the beginning and we will quickly go through all things.

39. It is indeed a difficult thing, to leave those things that are accustom, and present, and turn us to those things that are ancient, and according to the original.

40. For these things that appear delight us, but make the things that appear not, hard to believe.

4I. The things most apparent are Evil, but the Good is secret, or hidden, or to the things that appear for it has neither Form nor Figure.

42. For this cause it is like to itself, but unlike everything else; for it is impossible, that anything immaterial, should be made known, or appear to a Body.

43. For this is the difference between the like and the unlike, and the unlike wants always somewhat of the like.

44. For the Unity, Beginning, and Root of all things, as being the Root and Beginning.

45. Nothing is without a beginning, but the Beginning is of nothing, but of itself; for it is the Beginning of all other things.

46. Therefore it is, seeing it is not from another beginning.

47. Unity therefore being the Beginning contains every number, but it is contained of none, and produces every number, itself being produced of no other number.

48. Everything that is produced (or made) is imperfect, and may be divided, increased, diminished.

49. But to the perfect, there happens none of these.

50. And that which is increased, is increased by Unity, but is consumed and vanished through weakness, being not able to receive the Unity.

51. This Image of Amen, have I described to you, O Imhotep, as well as I could; which if you diligently consider, and view by the eyes of your mind, and heart, believe me, Son, you will find the way to the things above, or rather the Image itself will lead you.

52. But the spectacle or sight, has this peculiar and proper; Those that can see, and behold it, it holds fast and draws to it, as they say, the Loadstone Cloth Iron."

## The Thirteenth Book. "Of Sense and Understanding."

1. "Yesterday, Imhotep, I delivered a perfect Discourse; but now I think its necessary, in suite of that, to dispute also of Sense.

2. For Sense and Understanding seem to differ, because the one is material, the other essential.

3. But to me, they appear to be both one, or united, and not divided in men, I mean.

4. For in other living Creatures, Sense is united to Nature but in men to Understanding.

5. But the Mind differs from Understanding, as much as Amen from Divinity.

6. For Divinity is from or under Amen, and Understanding from the Mind, being the sister of the Word or Speech, and they the Instruments one of another.

7. For neither is the Word pronounced without Understanding, neither is Understanding manifested without the Word.

8. Therefore Sense and Understanding do both flow together into a man, as if they were infolded one within another.

9. For neither is it possible without Sense to Understand, nor can we have Sense without Understanding.

10. And yet it is possible (for the Time being) that the Understanding may understand without Sense, as they that fantasy Visions in their Dreams.

11.But it seems to me, that both the operations are in the Visions of Dreams, and that the Sense is stirred up out of sleep, to awaking.

12. For man is divided into a Body and a Soul; when both parts of the Sense accord one with another, then is the understanding simplified, or brought forth by the Mind pronounced.

13. For the Mind brings forth all Intellections or Understandings. Good ones when it receives good Seed from Amen; and the contrary when it receives them from Devils.

14. For there is no part of the World void of the Devil, which entering in privately, sowed the seed of his own proper operation; and the Mind did make pregnant, or did bring forth that which was sown, Adulteries, Murders, Striking of Parents, Sacrileges, Impieties, Strangling, throwing down recklessly, and all other things which are the works of evil Spirits.

15. And the Seeds of Amen are few but Great, and Fair, and Good Virtue, and Temperance, and Piety.

I6. And the Piety is the Knowledge of Amen, whom whoever knows being full of all good things has Divine Understanding and not like the Many.

17. And therefore they that have that Knowledge neither please the multitude, nor the multitude them, but they seem to be mad, and to move laughter, hated and despised, and many times also murdered.

18. For we have already said, that wickedness must dwell here, being in her own region.

19. For her region is the Earth, and not the World, as some will sometimes say, Blaspheming.

20. But the Faithful or Amen-worshipping Man laying hold on Knowledge will despise or tread under all these things; for though they be evil to other men, yet to him all things are good.

21. And on mature consideration, he refers all things to Knowledge, and that which is most to be wondered at, he alone makes evil things good.

22. But I return again to my Discourse of Sense.

23. It is therefore a thing proper to Man, to communicate and conjoin Sense and Understanding.

24. But every man, as I said before, cloths not enjoy, Understanding; for one man is material, another essential.

25. And he that is material with wickedness as I said, received from the Devils the Seed of Understanding; but they that are with the Good essentially are saved with Amen.

26. For Amen is the Workman of all things; and when He works He uses Nature.

27. He makes all things good like Himself.

28. But these things that are made good are in the use of Operation, unlawful.

29. For the Motion of the World stirring up Generations makes Qualities, infecting some with evilness, and purifying some with good.

30. And the World, Imhotep, has a peculiar Sense and Understanding, not like to Man's, nor so various or manifold, but a better and more simple.

31. For this Sense and Understanding of the World is One, in that it makes all things and unmakes them again into itself; for it is the Organ or Instrument of the Will of Amen.

32. And it is so organized or framed, and made for an Instrument by Amen; that receiving all Seeds into itself from Amen, and keeping them in itself, it makes all things effectually and dissolving them renews all things.

33.And therefore like a good Husband-man of Life, when things are dissolved or loosened, he affords by the casting of Seed, renovation to all things that grow.

34. There is nothing that it (the World) could not produce or bring forth alive; and by its Motion, it makes all things alive.

35. And it is at once, both the Place and the Workman of Life.

36. But the Bodies are from the Matter, in a different manner; for some are of the Earth, some of Water, some of Air, some of Fire, and all are compounded, but some are more compounded and some are simpler.

37. They that are compounded and are the heavier, and they that are less, are the higher.

38. And the swiftness of the Motion of the World makes the varieties of the Qualities of Generation, for the inspiration or influence, being most frequent, extends to the Bodies qualities with one fullness which is of Life.

39. Therefore, Amen is the Father of the World, but the World is the Father of things in the World.

40. And the World is the Son of Amen, but things in the World are the Sons of the World.

41. And therefore it is well called the World, that is an Ornament, because it adorned and beautifies all things with the variety of Generation and efficiency of Life, which the unwearied of Operation and the swiftness of Necessity with the mingling of Elements, and the order of things done.

42. Therefore it is necessarily and properly called the World.

43. For of all living things, both the Sense and the Understanding comes into them from without, inspired by that which encompasses them about, and continues them.

44. And the World receiving it once from Amen as soon as it was made, has it still, What Ever it Once Had.

45. But Amen is not as it seems to some who Blaspheme through superstit-ion, without Sense, and without Mind, or Understanding.

46. For all things that are, O Imhotep, are in Amen, and made by him, and depend on him; some working by Bodies, some moving by a Soul-like Essence, some quickening by a Spirit, and some receiving the things that are weary, and all very fitly.

47. Or rather, I say, that He has them not, but I declare the Truth, He is All Things, not receiving them from without, but exhibiting them outwardly.

48. And this is the Sense and Understanding of Amen, to move all things always.

49. And there never will be any time, when any of those things that are, will fail or be wanting.

50. When I say the things that are, I mean Amen, for the things that are, Amen has; and neither is there anything without Him, nor He without anything.

51. These things, O Imhotep, will appear to be true, if you understand them, but if you do not understand them seem incredible.

52. For to understand, is to believe, but not to believe, is not to understand; for my speech or words reach not to the Truth, but the Mind is great, and being led or conducted for a while by Speech, is able to attain to the Truth.

53. And understanding all things round about and finding them consonant, and agreeable to those things that were delivered and interpreted by Speech, believe; and in that good belief, rest.

54. To them, therefore, that understand the things that have been said of Amen, they are credible, but to them that understand them not, incredible.

55. And let these and so many things be spoken concerning Understanding and Sense."

## The Fourteenth Book. "Of Operation and Sense."

1. Imhotep: "You have well explained these things, Father: Teach me furthermore these things; for you say, that Science and Art were the Operations of the rational, but now you say that Beasts are unreason-able and for want of reason, both are and are called Brutes; so that by this Reason, it must need follow that unreasonable Creatures partake not of Science or Art, because they come short of Reason."

2. Tehuti: "It must need be so, Son."

3. Imhotep: "Why then, O Father, do we see some unreasonable living Creatures use both Science and Art? As the Ant treasure up for themselves food against the Winter, and Fowls of the Air likewise make them Nests, and four-footed Beasts know their own Dens."

4. "These things they do, O Son, not by Science or Art, but by Nature; for Science or Art are things that are taught, but none of these brutal Beasts are taught any of these things.

5. But these things being Natural to them are wrought by Nature, whereas Art and Science do not happen to all, but to some.

6. As men are Musicians, but not all; neither are all Archers or Huntsmen, or the rest, but some of them have learned something by the working of Science or Art.

7. After the same manner also, if some Pismires did so and some not, you might well say, they gather their food according to Science and Art.

8. But seeing they are all led by Nature, to the same thing, even against their wills, it is manifest they do not do it by Science or Art.

9. For Operations, O Imhotep, being actions, are in Bodies, and work by Bodies.

91

10. This is why, O Imhotep, in as much as they are actions, you must say they are immortal.

11. But in as much as they cannot act without Bodies, I say, they are always in a Body.

12. For those things that are to anything, or for the cause of anything made subject to Providence or Necessity, cannot possibly remain idle of their own proper Operation.

13. For that which is, shall ever be; for both the Body, and the Life of it, is the same.

14. And by this reason, it follows, that the Bodies also are always, because I affirm: That this corporeity is always by the Act and Operation, or for them.

15. For although earthly bodies be subject to dissolution; yet these bodies must be the Places, and the Organs, and Instruments of Acts or Operations.

16. But Acts or Operations are immortal, and that which is immortal, is always in Act, and therefore also Corporation if it be always.

17. Acts or Operations do follow the Soul, yet come not suddenly or promiscuously, but some of them come together with being made man, being about brutal or unreasonable things.

18. But the purer Operations do insensibly in the change of time, work with the oblique part of the Soul.

19. And these Operations depend on Bodies, and truly they that are Corporation come from the Divine Bodies into Mortal ones.

20. But every one of them act both about the Body and the Soul, and are present with the Soul, even without the Body.

21. And they are always Acts or Operations, but the Soul is not always in a Mortal Body, for it can be without a Body, but Acts or Operations cannot be without Bodies.

22. This is a sacred speech, Son, the Body cannot Consist without a Soul."

23. Imhotep: "How do you mean that, Father?"

24. Tehuti: "Understand it like this, O Imhotep, When the Soul is separated from the Body, there remained that same Body.

25. And this same Body according to the time of its death, it is dissolved and becomes invisible.

26. And these things the Body cannot do without, act or operation, and consequently there remained with the Body the same design of act or operation.

27. This then is the difference between an Immortal Body, and a Mortal one, that the immortal one consists of one Matter, but not the mortal one; and the immortal one acts, and does.

28. And everything that acts or operates is stronger, and rules; but that which is actuated or operated, is ruled.

29. And that which rules, directs and governs as free, but the other is ruled, as a servant.

30. Acts or Operations do not only actuate or operate living or breathing or en-souled Bodies, but also breathless Bodies, or without Souls, Wood, and Stones, and such like, increasing and hearing fruit, ripening, corrupting, rotting, putrefying and breaking, or working such like things, and whatever inanimate Bodies can do.

31. Act or Operation, O Son, is called, whatever is, or is made or done, and there are always many things made, or rather all things.

32 For the World is never widowed or forsaken of any of those things that are, but being always carried or moved in itself, it is in labor to bring forth the things that are, which will never be left by it to corruption.

33. Let therefore every act or operation be understood to be always immortal, in what manner of Body so ever it be.

34. But some Acts or Operations be of Divine, some of corruptible Bodies, some universal, some peculiar, and some of the generals, and some of the parts of everything.

35. Divine Acts or Operations therefore there be, and such as work or operate on their proper Bodies, and these also are perfect, and being on or in perfect Bodies.

36. Particular are they which work by any of the living Creatures.

37. Proper be they that work on any of the things that are.

38. By this Discourse, therefore, O Son, it is gathered that all things are full of Acts or Operations.

39. For if necessarily they be in every Body, and that there be many Bodies in the World, I may very well affirm, that there be many other Acts or Operations.

40. For many times in one Body, there is one, and a second, and a third, besides these universal ones that follow.

41. And universal Operations, I call them that are indeed bodily, and are done by the Senses and Motions.

42. For without these it is impossible that the Body should consist.

43. But other Operations are proper to the Souls of Men, by Arts, Sciences, Studies, and Actions.

44. The Senses also follow these Operations, or rather are the effects or perfections of them.

45. Understand therefore, O Son, the difference of Operations, it is sent from above.

46. But Sense being in the Body and having its essence from it, when it receives Act or Operation, manifested it, making it as it were corporeal.

47. Therefore, I say, that the Senses are both corporeal and mortal, having so much existence as the Body, for they are born with the Body, and die with it.

48. But mortal things themselves have not Sense, as Not consisting of such an Essence.

49. For Sense can be no other than a corporeal apprehension, either of evil or good that comes to the Body.

50. But to Eternal Bodies there is nothing comes, nothing departs; therefore there is no sense in them."

51. Imhotep: "Does the Sense therefore perceive or apprehend in every Body?"

52. Tehuti: "In every Body, O Son."

53. Imhotep: "And do the Acts or Operations work in all things?"

54. Tehuti: "Even in things inanimate, O Son, but there are differences of Senses.

55. For the Senses of things rational, are with Reason; of things unreasonable, Corporeal only, but the Senses of things inanimate are passive only, according to Augmentation and Diminution.

56. But Passion and Sense depend both on one head, or height, and are gathered together into the same, by Acts or Operations.

57. But in living things there be two other Operations that follow the Senses and Passions, to wit, Grief and Pleasure.

58. And without these, it is impossible that a living thing, especially a reasonable one, should perceive or apprehend.

59. And therefore, I say, that these are the Ideas of Passions that bear rule,

especially in reasonable living things.

60. The Operations work indeed, but the Senses do declare and manifest the Operations, and they being bodily, are moved by the brutal parts of the Soul; therefore I say, they are both malicious or doers of evil.

61. For that which affords the Sense to rejoice with Pleasure is straightaway the cause of many evils happening to him that suffers it.

62. But Sorrows gives stronger torments and Anguish, therefore doubtless are they both malicious.

63. The same may be said of the Sense of the Soul."

64. Imhotep: "Is not the Soul ethereal, and the Sense a Body, Father? Or is it rather in the Body?"

65. Tehuti: "If we put it in a Body, O Son, we will make it the Soul or the Operator, for these being disembodied, we say are in Bodies.

66. But Sense is neither Operation, nor Soul, nor anything else that belongs to the Body, but as we have said, and therefore it is not of substance.

67. And if it be not ethereal it must need be a Body; for we always say, that of things that are, some are Bodies and some ethereal."

## The Fifteenth Book. "Of Truth to His Son Imhotep."

1. Tehuti: "Of Truth, O Imhotep, it is not possible that man being an imperfect creature, compounded of imperfect Members, and having his Tabernacle consisting of different and many Bodies, should not speak with any confidence.

2. But as far as it is possible, and just, I say, That Truth is only in the Eternal Bodies, who's very Bodies be also true.

3. The Fire is fire itself only, and nothing else; the Earth is earth itself and nothing else; the air is air itself and nothing else; the water, water itself and nothing else.

4. But our Bodies consist of all these; for they have of the Fire, they have of the Earth, they have of the Water, and Air, and yet there is neither Fire, nor Earth, nor Water, nor Air, nor anything true.

5. And if at the Beginning our Constitution had no Truth, how could men either see the Truth, or speak it, or understand it only, except Amen would?

6. All things therefore on Earth, O Imhotep, are not Truth, but reflections of the Truth, even still not all things either; for they are but few that are so.

7. But the other things are Falsehood, and Deceit, O Imhotep, and Opinions are like the Images of the fantasy or appearance.

8. And when the fantasy has an influence from above, then it is a reflection of Truth, but without that operation from above, it is left a lie.

9. And as an Image shows the Body description, and yet is not the Body of that which it shows it to be, and it is seen to have eyes, but it sees nothing, and ears, but hears nothing at all; and all other things has the picture, but they are false, deceiving the eyes of the beholder, while they think they see the Truth, and yet they are indeed but lies.

10. As many therefore as see not Falsehood, see the Truth.

11. If therefore we do so understand and see every one of these things as it is, then we see and understand true things.

12. But if we see or understand anything besides or otherwise than that which is, we will neither understand, nor know the Truth."

13. Imhotep: "Is Truth therefore on Earth, O Father?"

14. Tehuti: "You could not miss the mark, O Son. Truth indeed is nowhere at all on Earth, O Imhotep, for it cannot be generated or made.

15. But concerning the Truth, it may be that some men, to whom Amen will give the good seeing Power, may understand it.

16. So that to the Mind and reason, there is nothing true indeed on Earth.

17. But to the True Mind and Reason, all things are fantasies or appearances, and opinions."

18. Imhotep: "Must we not therefore call it Truth, to understand and speak the things that are?"

19. Tehuti: "But there is nothing true on Earth."

20. Imhotep: "How then is this true, That we do not know anything true? How can that be done here?"

21. Tehuti: "O Son, Truth is the most perfect Virtue, and the highest Good itself, not troubled by Matter, not encompassed by a Body, naked, clear, unchangeable, venerable, unalterable Good.

22. But the things that are here, O Son, are visible, incapable of Good, corruptible, passable, dissolvable, changeable, continually altered, and made of another.

23. The things therefore that are not true to themselves, how can they be true?

24. For everything that is altered, is a lie, not abiding in what it is; but being changed it shows us always, other and other appearances."

25. Imhotep: "Is not man true, O Father?"

26. Tehuti: "For as far as he is a Man, he is not true, Son; for that which is true, has of itself alone its constitution and remains, and abides according to itself, such as it is.

27. But man consists of many things and does not abide of himself but is turned and changed, age after age, Idea after Idea, or form after form, and this while he is yet in the Tabernacle.

28. And many have not known their own children after a little while, and many children likewise have not known their own Parents.

29. Is it then possible, O Imhotep, that he who is so changed, is not to be known, should be true? No, on the contrary, he is Falsehood, being in many Appearances of changes.

30. But do you understand the true to be that which abides the same, and is Eternal, but man is not ever, therefore not True, but man is a certain Appearance, and Appearance is the highest Lie or Falsehood."

31. Imhotep: "But these Eternal Bodies, Father, are they not true though they be changed?"

32. Tehuti: "Everything that is produced or made, and changed is not true, but being made by our Progenitor, they might have had true Matter.

33. But these also have in themselves, something that is false in regard of their change.

34. For nothing that remains not in itself, is True."

35. Imhotep: "What should one say then, Father, that only the Sun which besides the Nature of other things, is not changed, but abides in itself, is Truth?"

36. Tehuti: "It is Truth, and therefore is He only entrusted with the Workman-ship of the World, ruling and making all things whom I do both honor, and adore His Truth; and after the One, and First, I acknowledge Him the Work-man."

37. Imhotep: "What therefore do you affirm to be the first Truth, O Father?"

38. Tehuti: "The One and Only, O Imhotep, that is not of Matter, that is not in a body, that is without Color, without Figure or Shape, Immutable, Unalter-able, which always is; but Falsehood, O Son, is corrupted.

39. And corruption has laid hold on all things on Earth, and the Providence of the True encompassed, and will encompass them.

40. For without corruption, there Generation cannot consist.

41. For Corruption followed every Generation that it may again be generated

42. For those things that are generated, must of necessity be generated of those things that are corrupted, and the things generated must need to be corrupted, that the Generation of things being, may not stand still or cease.

43. Acknowledge therefore the first Workman by the Generation of things.

44. Consequently the things that are generated of Corruption are false, as being sometimes one thing, sometimes another; for it is impossible they should be made the same things again, and that which is not the same, how is it true?

45. Therefore, O Son, we must call these things fantasies or appearances.

46. And if we will give a man his right name, we must call him the appearance of Manhood; and a Child, the fantasy or appearance of a Child; an

old man, the appearance of an old man; a young man, the appearance of a young man; and a man of ripe age, the appearance of a man of ripe age.

47. For neither is a man, a man; nor a child, a child; nor a young man, a young man; nor an old man, an old man.

48. But the things that pre-exist and that are, being changed are false.

49. These things understand so, O Son, as these false Operations having their dependence from above, even of the truth itself.

50. Which being so, I do affirm that Falsehood is the Work of Truth."

## The Sixteenth Book. "That None of the Things that are, can Perish."

1. Tehuti: "We must now speak of the Soul and Body, O Son; after what manner the Soul is Immortal, and what operation that is, which constitutes the Body, and dissolves it.

2. But in none of these is Death, for it is a conception of a name, which is either an empty word, or else it is wrongly called Death instead of Immortal.

3. For Death is destruction, but there is nothing in the whole world that is destroyed.

4. For if the World be a second Amen and an Immortal living Creature, it is impossible that any part of an Immortal living Creature should die.

5. But all things that are in the World are members of the World, especially Man, the reasonable living creature.

6. For the first of all is Amen, the Eternal and Unmade, and the Workman of all things.

7. The second is the World, made by Him, after His own Image and by Him holding together, and nourished, and immortalized; and as from its own Father, ever living.

8. So that as Immortal, it is ever living, and ever immortal.

9. For that which is ever living, differs from that which is eternal.

10. For the Eternal was not produced, or made by another; and if it were produced or made, yet it was made by itself, not by any other, but it is always made.

11. For the Eternal, as it is Eternal, is the Universe.

12. For the Father Himself is Eternal of Himself, but the World was made by the Father, ever living and immortal.

13. And as much Matter as there was laid up by Him, the Father made it all into a Body, and swelling it, made it round like a Sphere, endued it with Quality, being itself immortal, and having Eternal Materiality.

14. The Father being full of Ideas sowed Qualities in the Sphere, and shut them up, as in a Circle, Setting out to beautify with every Quality, that which should afterwards be made.

15. Then clothing the Universal Body with Immortality, lest the Matter, if it would change it state should be dissolved into its own disorder.

16. For when the Matter was immaterial, O Son, it was disordered, and it has here the same confusion daily revolved about other little things, endued with Qualities in point of Augmentation and Diminution, which men call Death, being indeed a disorder happening about earthly living creatures.

17. For the Bodies of Heavenly things have one order, which they have received from the Father at the Beginning, and is by the restoration of each of them, they are kept permanent.

18. But the restoration of earthly Bodies, is their consistence; and their dissolution restores them into permanence, that is, Immortal.

19. And so there is made a privation of Sense, but not a destruction of Bodies.

20. Now the third living creature is Man, made after the Image of the World; and having by the Will of the Father, a Mind above other earthly creature.

21. And he has not only relates with the second Amen, but also an understanding of the first.

22. For the second Amen, he takes as a Body but the first, he understands as Immaterial, and the Mind of the Good."

23. Imhotep: "And does not this living creature perish?"

24. Tehuti: "Speak advisedly, O Son, and learn what Amen is what the World is, what is an Immortal creature, and what a earthly One is.

25. And understand that the World is of Amen and in Amen; but Man is of the World and in the World.

26. The Beginning, and End, and Consist of all, is Amen."

## The Seventeenth Book. "To Imhotep, To Be Truly Wise."

1. Because my Son Imhotep, in your absence, would need to learn the Nature of the things that are: He would not suffer me to give over (as coming very young to the knowledge of every individual) till I was forced to discourse to him many things at large, that his contemplation might from point to point, be more easy and successful.

2. But to you I have thought good to write in few words, choosing out the principal heads of the things then spoken, and to interpret them more mystically, because you have, both more years, and more knowledge of Nature.

3. All things that appear, were made, and are made.

4. Those things that are made, are not made by themselves, but by another.

5. And there are many things made, but especially all things that appear, and which are different, and not like.

6. If the things that be made and done be made and done by another, there must be one that must make and do them; and He unmade and more ancient than the things that are made.

7. For I affirm the things that are made to be made by another; and it is impossible, that of the things that are made any should be more ancient than all, but only that which is not made.

8. He is stronger, and One, and only knowing all things indeed, as not having anything more ancient than Himself.

9. For He bears rule, both over multitude, and greatness, and the diversity of the things that are made, and the continuity of the Facture and of the Operation.

10. Moreover, the things that are made, are visible, but He is invisible; and for this cause, He makes them, that He may be visible; and therefore He makes them always.

11. So it is fit to understand, and understanding to admire, and admiring to think yourself happy that you know your natural Father.

12. For what is sweeter than a Natural Father?

13. Who therefore is this, or how will we know Him?

14. Or is it just to ascribe to Him alone, the Title and Glory of Amen, or of the Maker, or of the Father, or of all Three? That of Amen because of His Power; the Maker because of His Working and Operation; and the Father, because of His Goodness.

15. For Power is different from the things that are made, but Act or Operation in that all things are made.

16. Which is why, letting go all much and vain talking we must understand these two things, That Which is Made and Him Which is the Maker; for there is nothing in the middle, between these Two, nor is there any third.

17. Therefore understanding All things, remember these Two; and think that these are All things putting nothing into doubt; neither of the things above, nor of the things below; neither of things changeable, nor things that are in darkness or secret.

18. For All things are but two Things, That which Makes, and that which is Made, and the One of them cannot depart, or be divided from the Other.

19. For neither is it possible that the maker should be without the thing made, for either of them is the self-same thing; therefore cannot the One of them be separated from the other no more than a thing can be separated from itself.

20. For if He that makes be nothing else, but that which makes alone, Simple,

Uncompounded, it is of necessity, that He makes the same thing to Himself, to whom it is the Generation of Him that makes to be also All that is made.

21. For that which is generated or made must necessarily be generated or made by another, but without the Maker that which is made, neither is made, nor is; for the one of them without the other, has lost his proper Nature by the privation of the other.

22. So if these Two be confessed, That which makes and that which is made, then they are One in Union, this going before and that following.

23. And that which goes before, is, Amen the Maker, and that which follows is, that which is made, be it what it will.

24. And let no man be afraid because of the variety of things that are made or done, unless he should cast an aspersion of baseness, or infamy on Amen, for it is the only Glory of Him to do, or make All things.

25. And this making, or facture is as it were the Body of Amen, and to Him that makes or does, there is nothing evil, or filthy to be imputed, or There is Nothing thought Evil or Filthy.

26. For these are Passions that follow Generation as Rust does Copper, or as Excrements do the Body.

27. But neither did the Copper-smith make the Rust, nor the Maker the Filth, nor Amen the Evilness.

28. But the change of Generation does make them, as it were to blossom out; and for this cause did make Change to be, as one should say, The Purging of Generation.

29. Moreover, is it lawful for the same Painter to make both Heaven, and the Neter, and the Earth, and the Sea, and Men, and brutal Beasts, and inanimate Things, and Trees; and is it impossible for Amen to make these things? O the great madness and ignorance of men in things that concern Amen!

30. For men that think so, suffer that which is most ridiculous of all; for professing to bless and praise Amen yet in not ascribing to Him the making or doing of All things, they know Him not.

31. And besides their not knowing Him, they are extremely impious against Him, attributing to Him Passions, as Pride, or Oversight, or Weakness, or Ignorance, or Envy.

32. For if He does not make or do all things, He is either proud or not able, or ignorant, or envious, which is impious to affirm.

33. For Amen has only one Passion, namely Good and he that is good is neither proud, nor impotent, nor the rest, but Amen is Good itself.

34. For Good is all power, to do or make all things, and everything that is made is made by Amen, that is by the Good and that can make or do all things.

35. See then how He makes all things, and how the things are done, that are done, and if you will learn, you may see an Image thereof, very beautiful, and like.

36. Look at the farmer, how he caste Seeds into the Earth, here Wheat, there Barley, and elsewhere some other Seeds.

37. Look at the same Man, planting a Vine, or an Apple-Tree, or a Fig-Tree, or some other Tree.

38. So does Amen in Heaven sow Immortality, in the Earth Change in the whole Life, and Motion.

39. And these things are not many, but few, and easily numbered for they are all but four, Amen and Generation, in which are all things.

## The Eighteenth Book. "Of Auset the Virgin Mother."

**1.** Having thus spoken, Auset first pours out for Heru the sweet draught of immortality which souls receive from the Neter, and so begins the most holy discourse.

2. Heaven, crowned with stars, is placed above universal nature, O my son Heru, and nothing is wanting to it of that which constitutes the whole world. It is necessary, then, that all nature should be adorned and completed by that which is above her, for this Order could not proceed from below to above.

3. The supremacy of the greater mysteries over the lesser is imperative. Celestial order reigns over terrestrial order, as being absolutely determined, and inaccessible to the idea of death.

4. This is why, the things below lament, being filled with fear before the marvelous beauty and eternal permanence of the heavenly world.

5. For, indeed, a spectacle worthy of contemplation and desire were these glories of heaven, revelations of the Divine as yet unknown, and this sumptuous majesty of night illumined with a penetrating radiance, although less than that of the sun, and all these other mysteries which move above in harmonious cadence, ruling and maintaining the things below by secret influences.

6. And so long as the Universal Architect refrained from putting an end to this incessant fear, to these anxious investigations, ignorance enveloped the universe.

7. But when He judged good to reveal Himself to the world, He breathed into the Neter the enthusiasm of love, and poured into their mind the splendor which His bosom contained, that they might first be inspired with the will to seek, next with the desire to find, and lastly with the power to readjust.

8. Now, my wondrous child Heru, all this could not happen among mortals,

for as yet they did not exist; but it took place in the universal Soul in sympathy with the mysteries of heaven.

9. This was Tehuti, the Cosmic Thought. He saw the universe of things and having seen, he understood, and having understood, he had the power to manifest and to reveal.

10. That which he thought, he wrote; that which he wrote, he in great part concealed, wisely silent, and speaking by turns, so that while the world should last, these things might be sought. And so, having impressed on the Neter, his brethren, that they should follow in his path, he ascended to the stars.

11. But he had for successor his son, and the heir of his knowledge; Imhotep to by whom sovereign Providence reserved an exact knowledge of heavenly things.

12. Tehuti then justified himself in the presence of those who surrounded him, in that he had not delivered the integral theory to his son, on account of his youth. But I, having arisen, saw with my eyes, which see the invisible secrets of the beginnings of things, and at length, but with certainty, I understood that the sacred symbols of the cosmic elements were hidden near the secrets of Ausar.

13. Tehuti returned to heaven, having pronounced an invocatory speech. It is not fitting, O my Son, that this recital be left incomplete; you must be informed of the words of Tehuti when he laid down his books.

14. "O sacred books," he said, "of the Immortals, you in whose pages my hand has recorded the remedies by which incorruptibility is conferred, remain forever beyond the reach of destruction and of decay, invisible and concealed from all who frequent these regions, until the day will come in which the ancient heaven will bring forth instruments worthy of you, whom the Creator will call souls."

15. Having pronounced on his books this invocation, he wrapped them in their coverings, returned into the sphere which belonged to him, and all

remained hidden for a sufficient space.

16. And Nature, O my Son, was barren until the hour in which those who are ordained to survey the heavens, advancing towards the Divine, the King of all things, deplored the general inertia, and affirmed the necessity of setting forth the universe.

17. No other than He could accomplish this work. "We pray You," said they, "to consider that which already is, and that which is necessary for the future." At these words, the Divine smiled favorably, and commanded Nature to exist. And, issuing with His voice, the FEMININE came forth in her perfect beauty.

18. The Neter with saw this marvel with amaze. And the great Ancestor, pouring out for Nature an elixir, commanded her to be fruitful; and instantly, penetrating the universe with His glance, He cried, "Let heaven be the plenitude of all things, and of the air, and of the ether." The Divine spoke, and it was done. But Nature, communing with herself, understood that she might not transgress the commandment of the Father, and, uniting herself to Labor, she produced a most beautiful daughter, whom she called Invention, and to whom the Divine accorded being.

19. And having differentiated created forms, He filled them with mysteries, and gave the command of them to Invention.

20. Then, not willing that the upper world should be inactive, He saw fit to fill it with spirits, in order that no region should remain in immobility and inertia; and in the accomplishment of His work He used His sacred art.

21. For, taking of Himself such essence as was necessary, and mingling with it an intellectual flame, He combined with these other materials by unknown ways. And having achieved by secret formulas the union of these principles, He endowed with motion the universal combination.

22. Gradually, in the midst of the protoplasm, glittered a substance more subtle, purer, more limpid, than the elements from which it was generated. It was transparent, and the Artist alone perceived it.

111

23. Soon, it attained its perfection, being neither melted by the fire, nor chilled by the breath, but possessing the stability of a special combination, and having its proper type and constitution. He bestowed on it a happy name, and according to the similitude of its energies, He called it Self-Conscious-ness.

24. Of this product he formed myriads of Souls, employing the choicest part of the mixture for the end which He had in view, proceeding with order and measure, according to His knowledge and His reason.

25. The souls were not necessarily different, but the choicest part, animated by the Divine motion, was not identical with the rest.

26. The first layer was superior to the second, more perfect and pure; the second, inferior truly to the first, was superior to the third; and so, until sixty degrees, was completed the total number.

27. Only the Divine established this law, that which all equally should be eternal, being of one essence, whose forms He alone determines.

28. He traced the limits of their temporary stay on the heights of nature, so that they might turn the wheel according to the laws of Order and of wise discretion, for the joy of their Father.

29. Then, having summoned to these splendid regions of ether the souls of every grade, He said to them: "O souls, beautiful children of my breath and of my care, you whom I have produced with my hands, in order to consecrate you to my universe, hear my words as a law:--Quit not the place assigned to you by my will.

30. The abode which awaits you is heaven, with its galaxy of stars and its thrones of virtue. If you attempt any transgression against my law, I swear by my sacred breath, by that elixir of which I formed you, and by my creative hands, that I will speedily forge for you chains and cast you into punishment."

31. Having spoken so, the Divine, my Master, mingled together the rest of

the congenial elements, earth and water, and pronouncing certain powerful and mystic words—although different from the first--He breathed into the liquid protoplasm motion and life, rendered it thicker and more plastic, and formed of it living beings of human shape.

32. That which remained He gave to the loftiest souls inhabiting the region of the Neter in the neighborhood of the stars, who are called the Sacred Neter. "Work," said He, "my children, offspring of my nature; take the residue of my task, and let each one of you make beings in his image. I will give you models."

33. After that He took the constellations and ordained the world in conformity with –vital movements, placing the animal signs after those of human form.

34. And after having given forth the creative forces and generative breath for the whole range of beings yet to come, He withdrew, promising to unite to every visible work an invisible breath and a reproductive principle, so that each being might engender its similar without necessity to create continually new entities; and what did the souls do, O my Mother?

35. And Auset answered:--They took the mingled material, O my Son Heru, and began to reflect on it, and to adore this combination, the work of the Father.

36. Next, they sought to discover of what it was composed, which, indeed, it was not easy to find.

37. Then, fearing that this search might excite the anger of the Father, they set themselves to carry out His commands. Therefore, taking the upper portion of the protoplasm, that which was lightest, they created of it the race of birds.

38. The compound having now become more compact and assuming a denser consistency, they formed of it the quadrupeds; while of the thickest part which needed a moist vehicle for its support, they made fishes.

39. The remainder, being cold and heavy, was employed by the souls in the creation of reptiles. Immediately, O my Son, proud of their work, they were not afraid to transgress the Divine law, and, in spite of the prohibition, they receded from their appointed limits.

40. Not willing to remain longer in the same abode, they moved ceaselessly, and repose seemed to them death.

41. But, O my Son--(so Tehuti informed me)--their conduct could not escape the eye of the Lord the Divine of all things; He minded to punish them, and to prepare for them hard bonds.

42. The Ruler and Master of the universe resolved then for the penance of the souls, to mold the human organism, and having called me to Him, said Tehuti, He spoke in this way:--"O soul of my soul, holy thought of my thought, how long will earthly Nature remain sad? How long will the creation already produced continue inactive and without praise? Bring here before me all the Neter of heaven."

43. So the Divine spoke, quote Tehuti, and all obeyed His law. "Look on the earth," He said to them, "and on all things beneath," Straightaway they looked and understood the will of the Lord. And when He spoke to them of the creation of Man, asking of each what he could bestow on the race about to be born, the Sun first replied:--"I will illuminate mankind."

44. Then the Moon promised enlightenment in her turn, adding that already she had created Fear, Silence, Sleep, and Memory. Ma'at announced that she had produced Justice and Order. Ra said, "In order to spare the future race perpetual wars, I have generated Fortune, Hope, and Peace."

45. Set declared himself already father of Conflict, impetuous Zeal, and Emulation, Methur did not wait to be called on: "As for me, O Master," she said, "I will bestow on mankind Desire, with voluptuous Joy and Laughter, that the penalty, to which our sister Souls are destined may not weigh on them too hardly."

46. These words of Methur, O my Son, were welcomed gladly; "And I," said

Tehuti, "will endow human nature with Wisdom, Temperance, Persuasion, and Truth; nor will I cease to ally myself with Invention. I will ever protect the mortal life of such men as are born under my signs, seeing that to me the Creator and Father has attributed in the Constellations, signs of Knowledge and Intelligence; above all, when the movement which draws to it the stars is in harmony with the physical forces of each.

47. He Who is Master of the world rejoiced at hearing these things, and decreed the production of the human race. As for me--said Tehuti--I sought what material ought to be employed in the work, and invoked the Lord. He commanded the Souls to give up the residue of the protoplasmic substance, which having taken, I found it entirely dried up.

48. Therefore, I used a great excess of water with which to renew the combination of the substance, in such a way that the product might be resolvable, yielding, and feeble, and that Force should not be added therein to Intelligence.

49. When I had achieved my work it was beautiful, and I rejoiced in seeing it. And from below I called on the Lord to see what I had done. He saw it and approved. Straightaway He ordained that the Souls should be incorporated; and they were seized with horror on learning what should be their condemnation.

50. These words, said Auset, struck me. Listen, my son Heru, for I teach you a mystery.

51. Our ancestor Atum had it also from Tehuti, who inscribes the recital of all things; I, in turn, received it from the ancient One when he admitted me to the initiation of the black veil and you, likewise, O marvelous and illustrious child, receive it from me.

52. The Souls were about to be imprisoned in bodies, where at some sighed and lamented, as when some wild and free animal suddenly enchained in the first moment of subjection to hard servitude and of severance from the beloved habits of the wilderness, struggles and revolts, refusing to follow its conqueror, and if occasion presents itself, slaying him. Others, again, hissed

like serpents, or gave vent to piercing cries and sorrowful words, glancing aimlessly from height to depth.

53. "Great Heaven," said one, "principle of our birth, ether, pure airs, hands, and sacred breath of the sovereign the Divine, and you, shining Stars, eyes of the Neter, unwavering light of Sun and Moon, our early brethren, what grief, what rending is this!

54. Must we quit these vast, effulgent spaces, this sacred sphere, all these splendors of the paradise and of the happy republic of the Neter, to be precipitated into these vile and miserable abodes? What crime, O wretched ones, have we committed?

55. How can we have merited, poor sinners that we are, the penalties which await us?

56. See the sad future in store for us--to minister to the wants of a fluctuating and dissoluble body!

57. No more may our eyes distinguish the souls divine! Hardly through these watery spheres will we perceive, with sighs, our ancestral heaven; at intervals even we will cease altogether to behold it. By this disastrous sentence direct vision is denied to us; we can see only by the aid of the outer light; these are but windows that we possess--not eyes.

58. Nor, will our pain be less when we hear in the air the fraternal breathing of the winds with which no longer can we mingle our own, since that will have for its dwelling, instead of the sublime and open world, the narrow prison of the breast! But You, Who drives us forth, and causes us from so high a seat to descend so low, assign a limit to our sufferings!

59. O Master and Father, so quickly become indifferent to Your handiwork, appoint a term to our penance, deign to bestow on us some last words, while yet we are able to see the expanse of the luminous spheres!"

60. This prayer of the Souls was granted, my son Heru, for the Lord was present; and sitting upon the throne of Truth, He addressed them so: -- "O

Souls; you will be governed by Desire and Necessity; after me, these will be your masters and your guides. Souls subjected to my scepter which never fails, know that in as much as you remain stainless you will inhabit the regions of the skies. If among you any be found to merit reproach, they will inhabit abodes destined to them in mortal organisms. If your faults be light, you will be delivered from the bond of the flesh, and return to heaven.

61. But if you become guilty of graver crimes, if you turn away from the end for which you have been formed, then indeed you will dwell neither in heaven nor in human bodies, but from then on you will pass into those of animals without reason.

62. Having spoken so, O my son Heru, He breathed on them and said, "It is not according to chance that I have ordained your destiny; if you act ill, it will be worse; it will be better if your actions are worthy of your birth.

63. It is myself and not another who will be your witness and your judge.

64. Understand that it is because of your past errors that you are to be punished and shut up in fleshly bodies.

65. In different bodies, as I have already told you, your re-births will be different. Dissolution will be a benefit, restoring your former happy condition. But if your conduct be unworthy of me, your prudence, becoming blinded and guiding you backwards, will cause you to take for good fortune that which is really a chastisement, and to dread a happier lot as though it were a cruel injury.

66. The most just among you will, in their future transformations, approximate to the divine, becoming among men, upright kings, true philosophers, leaders and legislators, true seers, collectors of salutary plants, cunning musicians, intelligent astronomers, wise augurs, instructed ministrants: all beautiful and good offices; as among birds are the eagles which pursue not nor devour those of their own kind, and do not permit weaker ones to be attacked in their presence, because justice is in the nature of the eagle; among quadrupeds, the lion, for he is a strong animal, untamed by slumber, in a mortal body performing immortal toils, and by nothing tired

117

nor beguiled; among reptiles, the dragon, because he is powerful, living long, innocent, and a friend of men, allowing himself to be tamed, having no venom, and leaving old age, approximating to the nature of the Neter; among fishes, the dolphin, for this creature, taking pity on those who fall into the sea, will carry them to land if they still live, and will abstain from devouring them if dead, although it is the most voracious of all aquatic animals."

67. Having spoken these words, the Divine became an Incorruptible Intelligence.

68. After these things, my son Heru, there arose out of the earth an exceeding powerful Spirit, unencumbered with any corporeal envelope, strong in wisdom, but savage and fearful; although he could not be ignorant of the knowledge he sought, seeing the type of the human body to be beautiful and august of aspect, and perceiving that the souls were about to enter into their envelopes.

69. "What are these," said he, "O Tehuti, Secretary of the Neter?" "These are men," replied Tehuti. "It is a rash work," said he, "to make man with such penetrating eyes, such a subtle tongue, such a delicate hearing that can hear even those things which concern him not, such a fine scent, and in his hands a sense of touch capable of appropriating everything.

70. O generating Spirit do you think it is well that he should be free from care--this future investigator of the fine mysteries of Nature?

71. Will you leave him exempt from suffering--he whose thought will search out the limits of the earth?

72. Mankind will dig up the roots of plants, they will study the properties of natural juices, they will observe the nature of stones, they will dissect not only animals but themselves, desiring to know how they have been formed.

73. They will stretch forth their daring hands over the sea, and, cutting down the timber of the wild forest, they will pass from shore to shore seeking one another.

74. They will pursue the inmost secrets of Nature even into the heights, and will study the motions of heaven.

75. Nor is this enough; when nothing yet remains to be known than the furthest boundary of the earth, they will seek even there the last extremities of night.

76. If they apprehend no obstacle, if they live exempt from trouble, beyond reach of any fear or of any anxiety, even heaven itself will not arrest their audacity; they will seek to extend their power over the elements.

77. Teach them, then, desire and hope, in such a way that they may know likewise the dread of accident and of difficulty, and the painful sting of expectation deceived. Let the curiosity of their souls have for balance, desire and fear, care and vain hope.

78. Let their souls be a prey to mutual love, to aspirations and varied longings, now satisfied, now deceived, so that even the sweetness of success may be an allurement to draw them towards misfortune.

79. Let the weight of fevers oppress them, and break in them all desire."

80. You suffer, Heru, in hearing this your mother's recital? Surprise and wonder seize you in presence of the evils which now fall on poor humanity? That which you are about to hear is still more sad.

81. The speech of Heru pleased Tehuti; he deemed his advice good, and he followed it.

82. "O, Heru," said he, "the nature of the divine breath which enwraps all things will not be ineffectual! The Master of the universe has charged me to be His agent and overseer.

83. The Deity of the penetrating eye Ma'at will observe and direct all events; and for my part, I will design a mysterious instrument, a measure inflexible and inviolable, to which everything will be subject from birth even to final destruction, and which will be the bond of created entities.

84. This instrument will rule that which is on the earth, and all the rest."

85. It is so--quote Tehuti--that which I spoke to Heru; and instantly the instrument operated.

86. Straightaway the souls were incorporated, and I was praised for my work.

87. Then the Lord summoned anew the assembly of the Neter.

88. They gathered together, and He addressed them so: "Neter, who have received a sovereign and imperishable nature, and the sway of the vast eternity, you whose office it is to maintain unceasingly the mutual harmony of things, how long will we govern an empire unknown? How long will creation remain invisible to the sun and moon?

89. Let each of us undertake his part in the universe.

90. By the exercise of our power let us put an end to the cohesion of inertia.

91. Let chaos become a fable, incredible to posterity. Inaugurate your great labors; I will direct you."

92. He said, and immediately the cosmic unity, until now obscure, was opened, and in the heights appeared the heavens with all their mysteries.

93. The earth, so far unstable, grew more solid beneath the brightness of the sun, and stood forth adorned with enfolding riches.

94. All things are beautiful in the eyes of the Divine, even that which to mortals appears uncomely, because all is made according to the divine laws. And the Divine rejoiced in seeing His works filled with movement; and with outstretched hands grasping the treasures of nature. "Take these," He said, "O sacred earth, take these, O venerable one, who is to be the mother of all things, and from now on let nothing be lacking to you!"

95. With these words, opening His divine hands, He poured His treasures into the universal font.

96. But yet they were unknown, for the souls newly embodied and unable to support their opprobrium, sought to enter into rivalry with the celestial Neter, and, proud of their lofty origin, boasting an equal creation with these, revolted.

97. So men became their instruments, opposed to one another, and fomenting civil wars.

98. And so, force oppressing weakness, the strong burnt and massacred the feeble, and quick and dead were thrust forth from the sacred places.

99. Then the elements resolved to complain before the Lord of the savage condition of mankind.

100. For the evil being already very grievous, the elements hastened to the Divine the Creator, and pleaded in this way--the fire being suffered to speak first: "O Master," he said, "Maker of this new world, You whose name, mysterious among the Neter, has so far been revered among all men; how long, O Divinity, have You decreed to leave human life without the Divine?

101. Reveal Yourself to the world which calls for You, correct its savage existence by the institution of peace.

102. Grant to life, law, grant to night oracles; fill all things with happy auguries; let men fear the judgment of Amen, and no man will sin any more. Let crimes receive their just punishment, and men will abstain from unrighteousness. They will fear to violate oaths, and madness will have an end.

103. Teach them gratitude for benefits, so will I devote my flame to pure offerings and libations, and the altars will yield Thee exhalations of sweet savors.

104. For now I am polluted, O Master, because the impious temerity of men forces me to consume flesh.

105. They will not suffer me to remain in my nature; they pervert and corrupt my purity!"

106. The air spoke in its turn: "I am defiled by the effluvium of corpses, O Master; I am becoming pestilent and unwholesome, and from on high I witness things which I ought not to see."

107. Then the water took up the word, and spoke in this way, O my illustrious son:--"Father and wondrous Creator of all things, Divinity incarnate, Author of Nature who brings forth all through You, command the waters of the streams to be always pure, for now both rivers and seas are compelled to bathe the destroyer and to receive his victims!"

108. Then at the last the earth appeared, O my glorious son, and so began:-- "O King, Chief of celestial choirs and Lord of their orbits, Master and Father of the elements which lend to all things increase and decrease, and into which all must return; see how the impious and insensate the tribe of man overspreads me, O venerable One, since by Your commands I am the habitation of all beings, bearing them all and receiving into my bosom all that is slain; such is now my reproach.

109. Your terrestrial world in which all creatures are contained is bereft of the Divine. And because they revere nothing, they transgress every law and overwhelm me with all manner of evil works.

110. To my shame, O Lord, I admit into myself the product of the corruption of carcasses.

111. But I, who receive all things, would willingly also receive the Divine.

112. Grant to earth this grace, and if You come not as yourself for indeed I cannot contain You--let me at least receive some holy efflux of You.

113. Let the earth become the most glorious of all the elements; and since she alone gives all things to all, may she revere herself as the recipient of Your favors."

114. So the elements discoursed, and instantly the Divine filled the universe with His divine voice.

115. "Go," said He, "sacred offspring, worthy of your Father's greatness, seek not to change anything, nor refuse to my creatures your ministry.

116. I will send you an efflux of myself, a pure Being who will investigate all actions, who will be the dreadful and incorruptible Judge of the living; and sovereign justice will extend its reign even into the shades beneath the earth.

117. So will every man receive his merited deserts."

118. Immediately the elements ceased from their complaints, and each of them resumed its functions and its sway.

119. And in what manner, O my mother, said Heru, did the earth afterwards obtain this efflux of the Divine?

120. I will not recount this Nativity, said Auset; I dare not, O powerful Heru, declare the origin of your race, lest men in the future should learn the generation of the Neter. I will say only that the Supreme the Divine, Creator and Architect of the world, at length accorded to earth for a season, your father Ausar and the great mother Auset, that they might bring the expected salvation.

121. By them life attained its fullness; savage and bloody wars were ended; they consecrated temples to the Neter, their ancestors, and instituted oblations. They gave to mortal's law, nourishment, and raiment. "They will read," Tehuti said, "my mystic writings, and dividing them into two parts, they will keep certain of them, and inscribe on columns and obelisks those which may be useful to man."

122. Institutors of the first tribunals, they established everywhere the reign of order and justice.

123. With them began the faith of treaties, and the introduction into human

life of the religious duty of oaths.

124. They taught the rites of sepulture towards those who cease to live; they interrogated the horrors of death; they showed that the spirit from without delights to return into the human body, and that if the way of entry be shut against it, it brings about a failure of life.

125. Instructed by Tehuti, they engraved on hidden tables that the air is filled with Neter (hidden spirits).

126. Instructed by Tehuti in the secret laws of the Divine, they alone were the teachers and legislators of mankind, initiating them in the arts, the sciences, and the benefits of civilized life.

127. Instructed by Tehuti concerning the sympathetic affinities which the Creator has established between heaven and earth, they instituted religious representations and sacred mysteries.

128. And, considering the corruptible nature of all bodies, they ordained prophetic initiation, so that the prophet who lifts his hands to Amen should be instructed in all things, and that thereby philosophy and learning might provide nourishment for the soul, and medicine might heal the sufferings of the flesh.

129. Having performed all these things, O my son, and seeing the world arrived at its fullness, Ausar and I were recalled by the inhabitants of heaven; but we could not return there without having first praised the Lord, so that the celestial Vision might fill the expanse, and that the way of a happy ascension might open before us, since the Divine delights in hymns.

130. O my mother, said Heru, teach me this hymn, that I also may be instructed in it.

131. Listen, my son, answered Auset.

132. You have given me admirable instruction, O my most powerful Mother Auset, concerning the marvelous creation of Souls by the Divine, and

I am filled with wonder; but you have not yet shown me to what place souls depart when set free from bodies.

133. Willingly would I contemplate this mystery, and thank only you for the initiation.

134. And Auset said:--Listen, my son, for your most necessary inquiry holds an important place, and may not be neglected.

135. Hear my reply.

136. O great and marvelous scion of the illustrious Ausar, think not that souls on quitting the body mix themselves confusedly in the vague immensity and become dispersed in the universal and infinite spirit, without power to return into bodies, to preserve their identity, or to seek again their primeval abode. Water spilt from a vase returns no more to its place in it, it has no proper locality, it mingles itself with the mass of waters; but it is not so with souls, O most wise Heru. I am initiated into the mysteries of the immortal nature; I walk in the ways of the truth, and I will reveal all to you without the least omission.

137. And first I will tell you that water, being a body without reason, composed of myriads of fluid particles, differs from the soul which is, my son, a personal entity, the royal work of the hands and of the mind of the Divine, abiding herself in intelligence.

138. That which proceeds from Unity, and not from multiplicity, cannot mingle with other things, and in order that the soul may be joined to the body, the Divine subjects this harmonious union to Necessity.

139. Souls do not, then, return confusedly, nor by chance, into one and the same place, but each is dispatched into the condition which belongs to her. And this is determined by that which the soul experiences while yet she is in the tenement of the body, loaded with a burden contrary to her nature. Hear: therefore, this comparison, O beloved Heru; suppose that there should be shut up in the same prison, men, eagles, doves, swans, hawks, swallows, sparrows,

flies, serpents, lions, leopards, wolves, dogs, hares, oxen, sheep, and certain amphibious animals, such as seals, hydras, turtles, crocodiles, and that at the same moment all the creatures should be liberated.

140. All at once would escape; the men would seek cities and the public places, the eagles the ether, where nature teaches them to live, the doves the lower air, the hawks the higher expanse; the swallows would repair to places frequented by men, the sparrows to the orchards, the swans to districts where they could sing; the flies would haunt the proximity of the ground as high only as human exhalations extend, for the property of flies is to live on these and to flit over the surface of the earth; the lions and leopards would flee to the mountains, the wolves to the solitudes; the dogs would follow the track of man; the hares would betake themselves to the woods, the oxen to the fields and meadows, the sheep to the pastures; the serpents would seek the caves of the earth; the seals and the turtles would rejoin their kind in the shallows and running waters, in order to enjoy, conformably to their nature, alike the proximity of the shore and of the deep.

141. Each creature would return, conducted by its own interior discernment, into the abode befitting it.

142. Even so every soul, whether human or inhabiting the earth under other conditions, knows where she ought to go; unless, indeed, some son of Set should pretend that a bull may subsist in the waters or a turtle in the air. If, then, even when immersed in flesh and blood, souls do not infringe the law of order, although under penance--for union with the body is a penance--how much more will they conform to that place when delivered from their bonds and set at liberty!

143. Now this most holy law, which extends even to heaven, is in this way, O illustrious child: see the hierarchy of souls!

144. The expanse between the empyrean and the moon is occupied by the Neter, the stars, and the powers of providence. Between the moon and us, my son, is the abode of the souls.

145. The unmeasured air, which we call the wind, has in itself an appointed

way in which it moves to refresh the earth, as I will by and by relate. But this movement of the air on itself impedes not the way of the souls, nor does it hinder them from ascending and descending without obstacle; they flow across the air without mingling in it, or confounding themselves with it, as water flows over oil.

146. This expanse, my son, is divided into four provinces, and into sixty regions. The first province from the earth upwards comprehends four regions and extends as far as certain summits or promontories, which it is unable to transcend.

147. The second province comprises eight regions in which the motions of the winds arise.

148. Be attentive, my son, for you hear the ineffable mysteries of the earth, the heavens, and of the sacred fluid which lies between. In the province of the winds fly the birds; above this there is neither moving air nor any creature.

149. But the air with all the beings it contains distributes itself into all boundaries within its reach, and into the four quarters of the earth, while the earth cannot lift itself into the mansions of the air.

150. The third province comprehends sixteen regions filled with a pure and subtle element.

151. The fourth contains thirty-two regions, in which the air, fully subtle and diaphanous, allows itself to be penetrated by the element of fire.

152. Such is the order which, without confusion, reigns from depth to height to width, four general divisions, twelve intervals, sixty regions, and in these dwell the souls, each according to their nature.

153. They are indeed all of one substance, but they constitute a hierarchy; and the further any region is removed from the earth, the loftier is the dignity of the souls which dwell in it.

154. And now it remains to be explained to you, O most glorious Heru, what souls they are who abide in each of these regions, and this I will set forth, beginning by the most exalted.

155. The expanse which stretches between earth and heaven is divided into regions, my son Heru, according to measure and harmony. To these regions our ancestors have given various names; some call them zones, others firmaments, others spheres.

156. In them dwell the souls who are freed from bodies, and those who have not yet been incorporated.

157. The spaces which they occupy correspond with their dignity. In the upper region are the divine and royal souls; the baser souls--they who float over the surface of the earth—are in the lowest sphere, and in the middle regions are the souls of ordinary degree.

158. So, my son, the souls destined to rule descend from the superior zones, and when they are delivered from the body, there they return, or even higher still, unless indeed they have acted contrary to the dignity of their nature and to the laws of the Divine.

159. For, if they have transgressed, the Providence on high causes them to descend into the lower regions according to the measure of their faults; and in like manner also it conducts other souls, inferior in power and dignity, from the lower spheres into a more exalted abode.

160. For on high dwell two ministers of the universal Providence; one is guardian of the souls, the other is their conductor, who sends them forth and ordains for them bodies. The first minister guards them, the second releases or binds them, according to the will of the Divine.

161. In this way the law of equity presides over the changes which take place above, even as on earth also it molds and constructs the vessels in which the souls are immured.

162. This law is supplemented by two energies, Memory and Experience.

Memory directs in Nature the preservation and maintenance of all the original types appointed in heaven; the function of Experience is to provide every soul descending into generation with a body appropriate to it; so that passionate souls should have vigorous bodies; lazy souls lazy bodies; active souls active bodies; gentle souls gentle bodies; powerful souls powerful bodies; cunning souls dexterous bodies--briefly, that every soul should have a befitting nature.

163. For it is not without just cause that winged creatures are clothed with feathers; that intelligent creatures are gifted with finer senses and superior to others; that beasts of the field are furnished with horns, with tusks, with claws, or other weapons; that reptiles are endowed with undulating and flexible bodies, and lest the moisture of their natures should render them feeble, are armed either with teeth or with pointed scales, so that they are, even less than others, in peril of death.

164. As for fishes, these timid souls have allotted to them for a dwelling-place that element in which light is bereft of its double activity, for in the water, fire neither illuminates nor burns.

165. Each fish, swimming by the help of his spiny fins, flies where he wills, and his weakness is protected by the obscurity of the deep.

166. So are souls immured in bodies resembling themselves; in human shape, those souls who have received reason; in flying creatures, souls of a wild nature; in beasts, souls without reason, whose only law is force; in reptiles, deceitful souls, for they attack not their prey face to face, but by ambush; while fishes enshrine those timid souls who merit not the enjoyment of other elements.

167. In every order of animals there are individuals who transgress the laws of their being.

168. In what way, my Mother? said Heru. And Auset answered: In this way:--A man who acts against reason, a beast which eludes necessity, a reptile which forgets its cunning, a fish which loses its timidity, a bird which renounces freedom.

169. You have heard what was to be said concerning the hierarchy of souls, their descent, and the creation of bodies.

170. O my son, in every order of souls there are found a few royal souls, and of divers characters: some fiery, some cold, some proud, some gentle, some crafty, some simple, some contemplative, some active. This diversity belongs to the regions from where they descend into bodies.

171. From the royal zone the royal souls go forth, but there are many royalties; the royalty of spirit, of the flesh, of art, of science, of the virtues.

172. And how, said Heru, do you name these royalties?

173. O my son, the king of souls who has so far existed is your father Ausar; the king of bodies is the prince of each nation, he who governs.

174. The king of wisdom is the Father of all things; the Initiator is the thrice great Tehuti; over medicine presides Imhotep, the son of Tehuti; force and power are under the sway of Ausar, and after him, under yours, my son.

175. Philosophy depends on Tehuti; poetry, yet again, on Imhotep, son. So that, if you think about it, you will perceive that there are indeed many royalties and many kings.

176. But the supreme royalty belongs to the highest region; lesser kingships correspond to the spheres which bring them forth.

177. Those who issue from the fiery zone handle fire; those who come from the watery zone frequent liquid spheres; from the region of art and learning those are born who devote themselves to art and science; from the region of inactivity, those who live in ease and idleness. All that is done and said on earth has its origin in the heights, from where all essences are dispensed with measure and equilibrium; nor is there anything which does not emanate from above and returns there.

178. Explain to me this that you say, O my Mother.

179. And Auset answered:--An evident token of these exchanges has been stamped on all creatures by most holy Nature.

180. The breath which we indraw from the upper air we exhale and again inbreathe by means of the lungs within us which perform this work.

181. And when the way destined to receive our breath is closed, and then no longer do we remain on earth; we depart hence.

182. Moreover, O my glorious son, there are other accidents by which the balance of our combination may be destroyed.

183. What is, then, this combination, O my Mother?

184. It is the union and admixture of the four elements, from where emanates a vapor which envelops the soul, penetrates into the body and communicates to both its own character.

185. So are produced varieties among souls and bodies. If in the composition of a body, fire dominates, then the soul being already of an ardent nature, receives thereby an excess of heat which renders it the more energetic and furious, and the body the more vivacious and active. If the air dominates, the body and soul of the creature are thereby rendered unstable, errant and restless.

186. The domination of the water causes the soul to be mild, affable, bland, sociable, and easily molded, because water blends and mixes itself readily with all other things, dissolves them if it be abundant, moistens and penetrates them if it be less in quantity.

187. A body softened by too much humidity offers but a weak resistance, a slight malady disintegrates it, and little by little dissolves its cohesion.

188. Again, if the earthy element be dominant, the soul is obtuse, because the body lacks subtlety, nor can she force a way through the density of its organism.

189. Therefore, the soul remains indrawn on herself, borne down by the burden she supports, and the body is solid, inactive, and heavy, moving only with effort.

190. But if the elements be all in just equilibrium, then the whole nature is ardent in its actions, subtle in its motions, fluent in its sensations, and of a robust constitution.

191. Of the predominance of air and fire birds are born, whose nature resembles that of the elements which generate them. Men are endowed with an abundance of fire united with but a little air, and of water and earth equal parts. This excess of fire becomes sagacity, seeing that intelligence is indeed a kind of flame, which consumes not, but which penetrates.

192. The predominance of water and earth with a sufficient admixture of air and but little fire engenders beasts; those endued with more fire than the rest are the more courageous.

193. Water and earth in equal quantities give birth to reptiles, which being deprived of fire, have neither courage nor truthfulness, while the excess of water renders them cold, that of earth, sordid and heavy, and the lack of air makes all their movements difficult. Much water with but little earth produces fishes; the absence of fire and air in them causes their timidity, and disposes them to lie hidden, while the predominance of water and earth in their nature approximates them by natural affinity to earth dissolved in water.

194. Moreover, by means of the proportional increase of the elements composing the body is the body itself increased, and its development ceases when the full measure is attained.

195. And so long, my beloved son, as equilibrium is maintained in the primitive combination and in the vapors arising there from, that is, so long as the normal proportion of fire, air, earth, and water remains unchanged, the creature continues in health.

196. But if the elements deviate from the proportion originally determined--(I speak not now of the growth of activities, nor of that resulting from a change

of order, but of a rupture of equilibrium whether by addition or diminution of fire or of other elements)--then malady disruption.

197. And should air and fire, whose nature is one with that of the soul itself, prevail in the conflict, then, through the dominance of those elements, destroyers of the flesh, the creature abandons its proper state.

198. For the earthy element is the pabulum of the body, and the water with which it is permeated contributes to consolidate it; but it is the aerial element which confers motion, and the fire engenders all energies.

199. The vapors produced by the union and combination of these elements blending with the soul, as it were by fusion, bear her along with them, and clothe her in their own nature, whether good or evil.

200. So long as she remains in this natural association the soul keeps the rank she has attained. But if a change should occur either in the combination itself or in any of its parts or subdivisions, the vapors, altering their condition, alter likewise the relations between soul and body; the fire and air, aspiring upward, draw with them the soul, their sister, while the watery and terrestrial elements, which tend earthwards like the body, weigh it down and overwhelm it.

## The Ninetieth Book. "The Emerald Tablet"

1. **Here** is that which the priest Sagijus of Nabulus has dictated concerning the entrance of Balinas into the hidden chamber. **After my entrance into the chamber, where the talisman was set up, I came up to an old man sitting on a golden throne, who was holding an emerald tablet in one hand, and saw the following in Syriac, to the primordial language was written on it.**

2. Here is a truth, concerning which there can be no doubt.

3. It attests: As above is the below and the below from the above, all is the work of the miracle of the One.

4. And things have been from this primal substance through a single act. How wonderful is this work? It is the main (principle) of the world and is its maintainer.

5. Its father is the sun and its mother the moon.

6. The wind has borne it in its body, and the earth has nourished it.

7. The father of wonders and the protector of miracles.

8. Whose powers are perfect, and complete as a fire that becomes earth.

9. Separating the Earth from the fire, as the minor from the gross, with care and insight.

10. It rises from earth to heaven, so as to draw the lights of the heights to itself, and descends to the earth; so within it are the forces of the above and the below.

11. Because the light of lights is within it, so does the darkness flee before it.

12. The force of forces, which overcomes every subtle thing and penetrates into everything hard.

13. The structure of the microcosm is in accordance with the structure of the macrocosm.

14. And accordingly proceed the knowledgeable.

15. And to this aspired Tehuti, who was threefold graced with wisdom.

16. And this is his last book, which he concealed in the chamber.

## The Twentieth Book- "The 42 Divine Principles of Ma'at."

1. **I honor Amen.**

2. I have not committed violence.

3. I have not stolen.

4. I have not slain men or women

5. I feed the hungry.

6. I give offerings.

7. I have not defiled the sacred.

8. I have not told lies.

9. I have not been selfish.

10. I have not cursed.

11. I have not closed my ears to truth.

12. I have not committed adultery.

13. I honor animals as sacred.

14. I can be trusted.

15. I honor my community.

16. I give charity.

17. I remain in balance with my emotions.

18. I have not been a gossiper.

19. I honor my family.

20. I have not been angry without reason.

21. I have not disrupted families.

22. I have not polluted myself.

23. I communicate with compassion.

24. I have not disobeyed the Law.

25. I create harmony.

26. I have not cursed Amen.

27. I lead with love.

28. I am forgiving.

29. I have not acted hastily or without thought.

30. I have not overstepped my boundaries of concern.

31. I have not exaggerated my words when speaking.

32. I have not worked evil.

33. I have not used evil thoughts, words or deeds.

34. I have not polluted the water/land.

35. I have not spoken angrily or arrogantly.

36. I have not cursed anyone in thought, word or deeds.

37. I have not placed myself on a Pedestal.

38. I honor virtue.

39. I honor my ancestors.

40. I give guidance to children.

41. I advance through my own abilities.

42. I embrace life.

**Maa-Kheru (True of Voice/Action)**

**Legend Of Auser and Auset**

In the Pesedjet, Osiris is the husband of Isis, and brother of Set, all of whom are the great-grandchildren of the created god Atum, and Horus is not present within the system. In the Ogdoad, Osiris is not present within the system, and Horus is the husband of Isis and son of Ra, the creator god. When the Ennead and Ogdoad merged, Ra and Atum were identified as one-another, becoming *Atum-Ra*, and Horus was initially considered the fifth sibling of Osiris, Isis, Nephthys and Set. However, Horus' mother, Hathor, gradually became identified as a form of Isis, leading to Horus becoming said to be Isis' son, and therefore the son of Osiris.

Original legend

According to the original legend, Osiris was originally king over Egypt and civilized the nation with the assistance of Thoth's inventions of writing, law, the arts, and science. Having improved the Egyptians, Osiris traveled to other lands, placing Isis as his regent. However, Apep, the god of evil, was jealous and killed Osiris, so Isis had a son Horus from Osiris by inseminating his sperm, to avenge him. While young, Isis fled from Apep, a dangerous serpent, by hiding with Horus in the marshland of the Nile delta, where serpents would not follow. When Horus, a sun god, had grown up, he engaged in a great battle of light over the darkness of Apep, a battle so fierce that it was only ended when the other gods judged in Horus' favour and banished Apep.

There is strong evidence of the Biblical Adam and Eve corresponding to Atum and Isis and their sons Cain and Abel, and Seth to Osiris, Apep and Set.

Note the below article by Gary Greeber Author of such works as: *The Moses Mystery: The African Origins of the Jewish People* (Birch Lane Press, 1997), *The Bible Myth: The African Origins of the Jewish People* (Citadel Press, 1998, a paperback edition of *The Moses Mystery),* and *101 Myths of the Bible: How Ancient Scribes Invented Biblical History*

{The Theban doctrine holds that in the beginning there was the great primeval flood known as Nu or the Nun. The god Amen then appeared in a series of forms, first as an Ogdoad, then as Tatenen (a Memphite name for Imhotep identified with the primeval hill), then as Atum, who created the first gods, then as Re. After this he created humanity, organized the Ennead, appointed the four male members of the Hermopolitan Ogdoad as his divine fathers and priests, and appointed Shu as their leader. Another Theban tradition holds that Osiris built the first city at Thebes.

To equate all these ideas with the biblical Creation stories would be a massive undertaking, far beyond the scope of this short paper. Therefore I will deal only with a small piece of this very large subject. In this paper I will just compare some elements of the Heliopolitan cycle with the biblical account of Adam and Eve and the second day of Creation.

My point of departure is Genesis 2:4-5, which serves as a preamble to the story of Adam and Eve. Coming immediately after the account of the seven days of Creation, the text reads as follows:

*These are the generations of the heavens and of the earth when they were created, in the day that the LORD God made the earth and the heavens, and every plant of the field before it was in the earth, and every herb of the field before it grew: for the LORD God had not caused it to rain upon the earth, and there was not a man to till the ground.*

The phrase "generations of" appears eleven times in the Book of Genesis, but in the other ten instances it refers to stories about members of a family, such as in "the generations of Noah" or "the generations of Jacob." This indicates that the noun or nouns following after the words "generations of" refer to a parent or parents. Genesis 2:4, therefore, implies that "the heavens and the earth" are anthropomorphic beings with children, and that what follows is about the family of these two entities.

This formulation clearly implies a pagan throwback to the idea of Heaven and Earth as deities, but biblical scholars, determined to preserve the monotheistic view of biblical history, are reluctant to accept such an interpretation. Instead, they wrench the phrase out of context and assert that it simply means "things that are to follow" or "the history of."

A second major difficulty with Gen. 2:4-5 is the time frame in question. The passage indicates that the stories we are about to read take place "in the day that the Lord God made the earth and the heavens," and before the appearance of plant life. When is that day?

Biblical scholars tell us that the preamble refers to stories that take place after the seven days of Creation. But reading the passage literally and in context, it quite explicitly states that the stories we are about to read occurred on the day that God made the earth and the heavens and before the appearance of plant life. That time frame is clearly defined in the account of the seven days of Creation.

On the second day of Creation, a firmament arises out of the primeval waters and separates the waters above from the waters below. The biblical text says that the firmament came to be called "heaven." On the third day of Creation, the waters below gathered in one place to create the dry land, which was then called "earth," after which, plant life appeared. So the preamble to the story of Adam and Eve places the upcoming stories in the period between the division of the waters and the appearance of plant life, in the middle of the third day of creation.

Biblical scholars, however, note an interesting problem with this division between the second and third day. The second day is the only day in the sequence that isn't blessed by God. Instead, the third day receives two blessings, one after dry land or Earth appears, and one after the arrival of plant life. As many of these scholars have recognized, the gathering of the waters to create dry land continues the second day's process of rearranging and dividing the primeval waters. For this reason, they argue that the second day's blessing is held off to the middle of the third day because that is when the task of rearranging the primeval waters is finished. I would propose instead that the biblical redactor simply made an editing error, and the first half of Day Three actually belongs with Day Two and the associated blessing belongs at the end of Day Two. This would be consistent with the text of Genesis 2:4, which says that heaven and earth were created on the same day.

To summarize briefly, so far: On the second day of Creation, god placed a firmament in the primeval waters, separating the waters above from the waters below. The firmament was called Heaven. Then he gathered the waters below into a single place and created dry land. The dry land was called Earth. The preamble to the story of Adam and Eve places the starting point for the biblical stories on the second day of Creation, before the appearance of plant life on Day Three.

The arrangement of events on Day Two seems to closely parallel the Heliopolitan Creation myth. A great hill arose out of the primeval flood. This hill would obviously constitute a form of firmament. In some traditions that hill was Atum, the Heliopolitan Creator deity. In other traditions, Atum appeared at the top of the hill.

Atum, through act of masturbatory sex, brought forth two deities, Shu and Tefnut, representing "air" and "moisture". These two deities gave birth to the male deity Geb, who represented the earth, and the female deity Nut, who represented the heavens.

Several Egyptian pictures portray Shu as lifting Nut into the air and separating her from Geb. Sequentially, then, Atum appears as a firmament in the middle of the Nun and creates Shu who ultimately separates heaven and earth and symbolizes the space in between. Shu, therefore, becomes the firmament between Heaven and Earth.

Consider now how Genesis says the waters were divided. First, the waters above were divided from the waters below. Next, the waters below were gathered into a single place. "The waters above" is an Egyptian concept signifying the sky. We see it most clearly in images of the solar bark sailing through the heavens. Although Genesis says the firmament was called Heaven, I believe this was a late gloss by the biblical redactors. The firmament stands below the waters above. It is the waters above that would correspond to heaven. The firmament would be the space in between heaven and earth, corresponding first to the primeval mountain and then to Shu.

This brings us to the question of where in all the middle east would any people have such a concept as all the waters gathering in a single place, leaving fertile land behind in its retreat. The most logical location is the Nile River in Egypt. The gathering of the waters in one place is the primary Egyptian agricultural phenomenon. It derives from the annual overflowing of the Nile, which fertilizes the land and then withdraws, leaving the dry land in its place. For Egyptians, the Nile was the one and only great water way. Even the Mediterranean Sea attaches to the Nile.

Elsewhere, throughout Canaan and Mesopotamia, there were numerous large unconnected bodies of waters that were well known to the inhabitants of those lands. They include the Mediterranean Sea, Persian Gulf, Red Sea, Dead Sea, The Jordan River, the Tigris and The Euphrates. It is unlikely that the people of those lands would think of all these waters as gathering in a single place.

Returning to Genesis 2:4-5, we are told that when dry land was formed, no plant life existed because no man existed to till the ground. The next Genesis verses in sequence tell us: a mist rose up to water the dry land, God created "the Adam" out of the dust, (note that the bible says "the Adam", not "Adam"), then he planted a Garden and put "the Adam" in it. Observe here: 1) Adam appears before the plant life on Day Three and 2) that woman has not yet appeared. This is contrary to the sequence in the seven days of Creation, which places man and woman on the sixth day. Eve, or "the woman", which is how she is described until after the expulsion from the Garden of Eden, appears later in the sequence, after plants and after other animal life.

This arrangement strongly suggests that the man and woman created on Day Six were other than Adam and Eve, who appear earlier. The confusion arises from the fact that Adam and Eve originally represented Heliopolitan deities, the most important of whom was named Atum, a name virtually identical in pronunciation to the Semitic word "Adam", which was used to describe the human male. The later biblical redactors, unable to conceive of Adam and Eve as deities, thought of them instead as the first humans, and equated them with the man and woman created on Day Six, who actually are the first humans in the Genesis Creation story.

Chronologically and contextually, we see that Genesis introduces Adam and Eve as the anthropomorphic beings referred to in Genesis 2:4 as heaven and earth, and since Adam is created out of the dust of the earth, we can equate him with the Egyptian deity Geb or Earth and we can equate Eve with the Egyptian deity Nut or heaven.

Eve enters the story, however, only after she is physically ripped from the body of Adam. This separation of Adam (the earth) from Eve (the Heaven) closely parallels the Egyptian account in which Shu physically pulls Heaven from the Earth. It also incorporates the Heliopolitan idea that a male and female deity were created from a single male deity.

There are some other interesting parallels between Geb and Nut and Adam and Eve. According to Plutarch's account of the Osiris myth, Re, the chief deity, ordered Geb and Nut not to couple. They disobeyed his injunction and were punished. Re ordered Shu to

141

separate the two bodies and declared that Nut would not be able to give birth on any day of the year. Thoth, sympathetic to Nut's plight, won some light from the Moon and created five new days. Since these days were not yet part of the year, Nut could give birth on these five days. She had five children, one on each day, born in the following order: Osiris, Horus, Set, Isis and Nephthys, the three males first and then two females. The Egyptians memorialized this sequence in their calendar, which names the last five days of the year after these five deities in the order of their births. Because of the role of Geb and Nut in birthing these deities, they were often known as the father and mother of the gods.

Observe the sequence of events: The chief deity gives a direct command to Heaven and Earth. They violate the order and as a penalty the chief deity makes child birth a painful act for the female. Subsequently she gives birth to three sons. As we know from other Egyptian myths, one of those three sons, Set, kills one of the other sons, Osiris.

Genesis has a similar plot. God gives Adam and Eve (or Earth and Heaven) a direct order. They disobey that order and one of the punishments inflicted includes pains with child birth. Subsequently, Eve gives birth to three sons named, Cain, Abel, and Seth, one of whom kills one of the other brothers. Also, Eve is identified in the bible as the "mother of all living", an identification similar to Nut's designation as mother of the gods. So, as with Nut, Eve disobeys God, is punished with pain in childbirth, has three male sons, one of whom kills one of the others, and she is thought of as the first mother.

Interestingly, the Hebrew name Seth and the Egyptian name Set are philologically identical and both children are born third in sequence. However, as some will note, in the biblical sequence it is not Seth who kills his brother. Instead, Cain does the killing. Cain, as the oldest brother, should correspond to Osiris and his killing of another brother is inconsistent with the Egyptian story. Why that occurs is too complex an issue to be resolved in this paper and we will let it pass. However, a little further below, we will see that Cain and Osiris share some other characteristics.

Although Adam and Eve start out as Geb and Nut they also share some aspects of Osiris and Isis. In this regard, we should observe that the Egyptians recognized a deity known as Geb-Osiris who was thought to have created the cosmic egg in Hermopolitan creation myths. Therefore, a merging of Geb and Osiris into a single character involved with Creation does not undermine the theme of this paper. However, I should observe that I believe the biblical character of Adam initially corresponds to the Egyptian god Atum and that Genesis incorporates within Adam all the members of the Ennead. This is consistent with the Egyptian view of Atum, who was also thought of as including within himself all the members of the Ennead.

The connection between Adam and Eve and Osiris and Isis is most apparent in the story of the serpent and the forbidden fruit. Osiris, as ruler of the afterlife, had to make two decisions with regards to the people who appeared before him. First he had to decide if the person lived a moral life; then he had to determine whether to grant that individual eternal life.

In Genesis, we learn that the Garden of Eden had two special trees. The fruit of one gave knowledge of good and evil; the fruit of the other gave eternal life. Thus, the ability of Adam to have control over the fruit of these trees would give him the same status as Osiris, but the biblical theology can not allow an Osiris to exist, so access to those fruits were forbidden by the one true deity. The nature of this conflict is even noted in the bible when God says to one of his angels, "Behold, the man is become as one of us, to know good and evil: and now, lest he put forth his hand, and take also of the tree of life, and eat, and live for ever:"

I suppose almost everyone who reads the story of Adam and Eve has at one time or another questioned why it was such a terrible thing for these two people to learn about the difference between good and evil. I suggest that to ask this question is to misunderstand what the story was really about. The story was not about good and evil. It was about the need to diminish the role of Osiris as a school figure.

As a consequence of Adam and Eve eating the fruit, God administered some punishments. We have already mentioned the problem of childbirth. In addition, Adam lost his kingdom and was banished from the Garden. He journeyed to a new land where he became a farmer who had to suffer hard labor in order to produce food. As to the serpent who tricked Adam into losing his kingdom, God declared that there should be enmity between the woman and the serpent and between her seed and his seed. Furthermore, the seed of the woman shall bruise the head of the serpent and the serpent shall bruise the heel of the woman's seed.

Again, these themes seem to be drawn from the Osiris cycle. In the Osiris myth, especially as related by Plutarch, Osiris and Isis ruled in a golden age. Osiris traveled far and wide teaching the people what he knew and Isis ruled in his absence. But the god Set, whom the Egyptians frequently identified with the serpent Apep, enemy of Re, conspired to take the throne for himself. Through trickery, he trapped Osiris in a chest, killed him, and hid the box away. Subsequently, Set hacked the body into pieces and buried them around the land of Egypt. Isis, fearing for the safety of Horus, her child, hid him away from Set. Still, Set managed to sneak up on Horus, and in the form of a serpent bit at his heel. But for the intervention of the gods, Horus would have died. When Horus grew up he avenged his father's murder and defeated Set in battle.

In Genesis, the Osiris role is shared between Adam and Cain. For comparisons, we begin with the observation that the key scene in the Garden of Eden involves a serpent in a tree trying to kill Adam by tricking him into eating the forbidden fruit. The trick worked. Where Adam was essentially a fertile agricultural deity in the Garden of Eden, he has now been figuratively killed in that he now lives as a mortal and he must sweat out agricultural growth. He no longer rules as king in a golden age.

Indeed, the bible implicitly recognizes that the serpent killed Adam. The text explicitly says that if Adam ate from the Tree of Knowledge of Good and Evil he would surely die. Since the serpent tricked Adam into committing this life extinguishing act, he has, like Set, killed the king. That Adam didn't actually die in accord with the warning is no doubt due to the confusion of identities in later times between Adam and Eve and the first man and woman created on Day Six.

As to the serpent who tricked Adam, just as Set tricked Osiris, he and Eve became enemies, just as Set and Isis became enemies. Also, just as Set bit the heel of Horus, Genesis said that the serpent would bruise the heel of Eve's children. And just as Horus avenged Set by beating him in battle, Genesis says that the seed of Eve will bruise the head of the serpent.

With regard to this last matter, let me call your attention to a well-known Egyptian scene generally identified as "The Great Cat of Heliopolis". It shows a cat with a stick bruising the head of a serpent who is sitting in a tree. Egyptologists usually identify the Cat as Re and the serpent as Apep his enemy. Ichnographically, while the Great Cat scene no doubt derives from the conflict between Re and Apep, the image portrayed seems remarkably consistent with the biblical story of Adam and Eve. I suspect that if we replaced the Cat with a more human image of one of the sun Gods, Re, Atum, or Horus, and left out the identifying words, many persons unfamiliar with the origin of the picture might consider it an illustration for the story of Adam and Eve.

As noted above, Cain as the oldest of Eve's three children should correspond to Osiris, and many such correspondences exist. To begin with, like Osiris, Cain is an agricultural figure associated with fruit farming. Osiris wandered far and wide spreading his knowledge and teachings. Cain also wandered far and wide spreading his knowledge and teachings. In fact, Cain's name is Semitic for "smith", a craft figure, and Cain's descendants, according to Genesis, are the founders of all the creative arts and sciences.

In Theban tradition, Osiris built Thebes, which was the first city. According to Genesis, Cain also built the first city. He built it in a land called Nod. Curiously, the bible refers to the city of Thebes by the name "No", a rather close philological fit with "Nod".

Finally, although we noted the anomaly of having Cain, the Osiris character, kill his brother instead of having the brother corresponding to Set do the killing, we do note that in both the Egyptian and biblical stories, we appear to have the story of the first murder and in each instance the killer buries the body and hides it from view, in the hope that no one will discover it.

In conclusion, I note that the bible places Israel's formative years as a scholarly entity in Egypt, and its leading figures, Joseph and Moses, were educated in Egypt's traditions. What they knew about the origins of the world they learned in Egypt, and what they wrote about those origins should surely have had an Egyptian influence.

Yet, while scholars are willing to admit all sorts of Semitic pagan influences on early Hebrew historical beliefs, they treat the idea of Egyptian influence as far too profane for intense examination. I hope in this paper I have been able to at least raise some interest in more closely examining the idea that Egyptian ideas greatly influenced the writing of early biblical history.}

Originally, Osiris' death was blamed on Apep, but after the time of the foreign Hyksos invaders-overlords (at the end of the Middle Kingdom), Set, the favorite god of the Hyksos, was increasingly viewed by the Egyptians as an evil god, having originally been a hero, and so the blame was transferred to Set. The Hyksos (Egyptian heka khasewet/ rulers of foreign lands) were an ethnically mixed group of Southwest Semitic Asiatic people who appeared in the eastern Nile Delta during the Second Intermediate Period.

At the time the myth initially developed, it was believed that the gods had emerged from under the acacia tree owned by Iusaaset, Atum's shadow, requiring an explanation of how Horus came to be born at the tree. Thus the original form of the myth states that Osiris was killed by a wooden sarcophagus secretly being made to his measurements, and then a party held where the coffin was offered to whoever it fitted. A few people tried to fit in, but to no avail, until Osiris was encouraged to try, who, as soon as he lay back, had the lid slammed on him and it sealed closed. The coffin was thrown into a river, causing Osiris to drown, but the coffin eventually was rescued by Isis and Nepthys, who used magic to bring life to Osiris/Horus inside. The coffin sprouted greenery, eventually turning into an acacia tree, from which the newly young Horus emerged.

The act of evil in drowning Osiris was said to have been the work of 72 unnamed conspirators, reflecting the legend in which 1/72nd of the moon's light was said to have been won by Thoth for the birth of the five major gods - Set, Nepthys, Osiris, Isis, and Horus, each 1/72nd of the moon's light given for the five days reflecting an individual piece of darkness left in its place during the 360. This legend was itself based on the fact that 1/72 over 360 days, the length of the year in the older Egyptian calendar, produces 5 whole days, reflecting the duration of the newer 365 day Egyptian calendar.

In late Egyptian thought, the righteous dead were sometimes honored by association to the stars, and thus the moon was occasionally seen as having a connection to Osiris, lord of the dead. As a death and resurrection legend, in which evil seeks to destroy a deity, thus bringing darkness, it thus developed an association with the lunar cycle, in which the moon appears to be destroyed by darkness, and is then brought back to life. Thus it later became said that Osiris had been killed by being dismembered into 13 parts, each part representing one of the 13 full moons seen each year (there are roughly 13 lunar months per year). The original form of Set's murder of Osiris was incorporated into this later version, though it was said that the attempt had failed when Isis and Nepthys found the coffin and rescued it.

However, the resurrected form was Horus, who had previously been considered a sun-god, having been identified with Ra as *Ra-Herakhty*, and the solar *death-resurrection* cycle over a year involves a whole entity, said to be composed of 12 sections - the zodiac.

Consequently, it became said that before resurrecting Osiris/Horus, Isis put together 12 of the 13 parts, but was unable to find the 13th, which was said to have been destroyed completely. As Set was considered to be homosexual (due to having originally been the god of the desert, and thus thought of as infertile), it was said that a manifestation of Set - the Oxyrhynchus fish (a fish with an unusual curved *snout* resembling depictions of Set), had swallowed the part that was Osiris' penis.

As a life-death-rebirth deity, Horus/Osiris became a reflection of the annual cycle of crop harvesting as well as reflecting people's desires for a successful afterlife, and so the legend became extremely important, outstripping all others. The legend's ventures into both life and afterlife meant that religious rites associated with the legend eventually began to take on aspects of a mystery school, where initiates were said to be able to partake in Horus/Osiris' resurrection, purging themselves of past ills, and entering a new life, i.e. "being born again".

In Greece, the Demeter-Persephone death-resurrection school at Eleusis, had a similar nature, and began at an extremely similar time. Many centuries later this led to interest in the Egyptian school by the Greeks, including Plato. Eventually, a derived form of the Egyptian school, having been infused with Platonism, spread to areas of Greek influence, particularly during the Hellenic era of control over Egypt. As the school referred to foreign gods, the forms of the school in Greek nations were adopted to describe suitable local deities and merged and expanded to include elements from the local scholars. This produced a collection of closely related versions of the school, whose central deities had been deformed to be similar to the Egyptian school, and were by the 1st century BC collectively known as Osiris-Dionysus, Demeter, Greek goddess of the harvest.

### Influences

Some scholars and researchers (including some skeptical of the actuality of early Christian accounts) have argued that there are similarities and parallels between the story of Osiris, and later Christian stories, such as the story of the resurrection of Jesus or of Lazarus. Furthermore, some suggest that the earlier Egyptian tales influenced and helped shape the later Christian accounts. Christ being from the Egyptian Krst a title meaning Anointed One. In addition, the original written spelling of Lazarus was given in Koine Greek as "Lazaros", which has been suggested as a corruption of "El-Azar-Os". This is a Hebrew theophoric prefix and a Graecizing suffix, and as a whole is cognate with Osiris, who was originally called *Azar*. The name *Osiris* itself has a similar etymology - it is the Greek transcription of the original Demotic script name *Azar*, with an additional Graecizing suffix of *is* (i.e. *Azar-is*). It's also been argued that there are parallels between Jesus and Horus, and that they are syncretistic.

## Culture

Ancient Egypt, much like today, was a mix of peoples and cultures. Up to the Hyksos/Hittite era it was undoubtedly African Black People. Although this is area for debate in the western world due to racism and scholarly and historical mistakes and outright lies. There are countless descriptions, signifiers and depictions of them in the historical record ranging from paintings, cosmetics, culture, and Greek and Persians written accounts of them being dark tone and woolen haired.

In addition their descendents are still living there and the name Egypt is an abbreviation of Ethiopia, which is Greek for "Land of the burn face" as well as the Sudan which is Arabic for Land of the Blacks. Present day Sinai, Egypt, Ethiopia and Sudan/Nubia: at one time in history where states, vassals, or territories of what is called Egypt. A clearer picture of migration would be from the upper Nile valley (Nubia) through the lower Nile valley (Modern Egypt) to the Fertile Crescent (Sinai, Israel, Palestine part of Syria and lower Turkey) (in fact Syria still bears the name of Osiris to this day). Because the Nile River flows south to north, Upper Egypt is down and Lower Egypt is up.

The historical record shows that the Egyptian culture began in Upper Egypt closer to present day Sudan/Nubia and migrated along the Nile River due north. Over time there where encounters with other tribes and cultures, and so two separate groups emerged sharing a common history but different perspective. This is the genesis of the Upper and Lower Kingdoms or the Two Crowns. When Namer (the Scorpion King) united the two lands; so rose the First Dynasty and the beginning of reunifying the two crowns and common yet distinct cultures. This is the reason for differences, overlap and similarities of the names of the ancestors and or deities in their written record.

In ancient Egypt government power rest with the different schools who associated with a different ancestor or deity, similar to the US republican Elephant or Democrat Donkey, difference being in ancient Egypt there was no division for religion and government. They did not look at religion as we do today, it would be more accurate to say away of life. Imagine the Shaolin Buddhist and the Wu-tang Buddhist running China's government and both with the same base doctrine but overtime developed different perspectives, and the group in power would showcase their point of view from their cultural perspective. This is a simplification of a much more complex social governing system that modified and adapted to last over ten thousands years and some speculate much older.

Recently in Ethiopia/Eritrea you have cultural groups such as the Eritreans, Tigray, Amahara and Oromo, most share a similar language and culture but see themselves as unique and different. Although Amharic is the official language of Ethiopia the Oromo are the oldest and largest group of people in the region. The Tigray and Amhara languages derive from Ge'ez and the Oromo language derives from Cushite. Like the ancient Egyptians these cultural groups of Ethiopia/Eritrea share a common and strong connection to community and family and it reflects in their overall philosophy.

There are many more cultural groups and languages in Ethiopia/Eritrea all have lived together for thousands of years; they share similar origins but have different cultures and perspectives. With out the help of camels or horses it takes the average person one day to walk twenty miles, in ancient times most people lived and worked in a ten mile radius. But as the population grew and ships and navigation advanced, the Egyptians reunited and spread throughout the globe trading goods and services and sharing knowledge and ideals. There is hardly a continent on earth that their presence is not recorded. And it's with these truths and legacy we seek their gift of resurrection to walk again as the elders of men. Hotep

## Glossary

Amen- (Amon, Amin, Amun, Amma, Nyame) The hidden one, The all, One god, The creator.

Atum- (Adam, Demu, Temu) which means to complete or finish.

Ausar- (Aser, Osiris, Cyrus, Sirius, Lazarus) Rebirth, The Resurrected One. Spring. Vegetation.

Auset- (Isis, Ishtar) She of the Throne. The nourishing Mother.

Bemaa - Alter

Geb – (Seb, Keb) Weak one, Drunkard, Possible association with Noah.

Heru – (Horus, Hero, Hercules,) Immaculate son of Ausar and Asuset, The Protector, Overseer, Hawk .

Het-Hu -Temple

Het-nen-nesu – (Herakleopolis Magna) House of the royal child.

Imhotep (Idris, Enoch) - One who comes in peace. He is considered the first polymath-a person whose knowledge is not restricted to one subject area. In less formal terms, a polymath (or polymathic person) may simply refer to someone who is very knowledgeable. Most ancient scientists were polymaths by today's standards.

Isfet- (Apep, Apophis,) Evil, Chaos, Devil, Python Snake,Crocodile

Kemet (Egypt) Land of the blacks.

Ma'at- Truth, balance, order, law, morality, and justice— sometimes personified as a goddess. Regulating the stars, seasons, and the actions of both mortals and the deities, who set the order of the universe from chaos at the moment of creation.

Methur- (Hathor, Mother,) House of Horus. The Milky Way Galaxy, The Nile, Great Cow.

Min-(Khem+Amin) The black one. The maker of all, Fertilizer, Originator.

Ineb Hedj- (Memphis) The White Walls

Iterw (Nile, ) The River

Neter – (Nature) Forces, Spirits, Divine

Nebet-het – (Nepthys) Lady of the House sister of Isis.

149

Nebu – (Nubia,) Word for gold

Nut – (Nuit, Newet) Night Bearer. Associated with rain. Companion to Geb.

Octonary- Eight elements, as in the bible eight cubits.

Ogdoad – Greek for group of eight deriving from Pesedjet.

Pesedjet- Reunited Rulers (Ennead Greek for group of nine)

Ptah (Peteh, Peter) The Risen land, or the rock

Ra- (Re, Ray) The Sun, Fire, Power

Sesen- Water Lily or Lotus Greek Pomander – Current Era- Holy Spirit

Set- (Seth, Shatan, Satan) He who dazzles. Lord of Struggle. The desert.

Ta-Iterw- (Nile Valley) Land of the River

Ta-Seti (Nubia, Sudan) As referred to by Kemet "Land of the bow".

Tehuti- (Thoth) He who is like the ibis" Master of Knowledge.


**Sources/ Latin Name**

The Corpus Hermiticum -Books 1-17

Kore Kosmou -Book 18

The Emerald Tablet -Book 19

The 42 Negative Confessions -Book 20

The Generations of the Heavens and of the Earth: Egyptian Deities in the Garden of Eden
*Presented at the annual meeting of the American Research Center in Egypt, St. Louis 1996*
By Gary Greenberg

NationMaters.com

WikiPedia.com

Self Education

# The Shat-Nesu Enderase

Interpreted by Ras-Nahmir Amun

ISBN - 978-0-9885163-1-1

**Secound Edition**

# Table of Contents

## The Shat-Nesu Enderase
*(The Books of Kings and Viziers)*

Forward

The name for king in Kemet was not Nesu which is a Greece corruption of
the title SMR PAR meaning -Great House-. More regularly they would have
been referred to as Nesut (his Majesty) or Nesu-Bit (King of the two lands)
this is still echoed today in the royal title for king in Ethiopia – Negus. A
spiritual leader and commander, the Nesu was a shepherd to his people; the
measure and weigh for all Kemet. Nesu's ruled with a Vizier; in Kemet
referred to as Tjati and echoed as Enderase in Ethiopia. Tjati typically where
a Prince and or high priest serving as counsel to the Nesu; and second in
command in Kemet. Imhotep was one of the greatest of Tjati together with
Nesu Dojser they guided Kemet through a golden age and forever changed
the world.

A society is judged by its government and criminals for both are of the
people. When the government is of the people, for the people, and by the
people, it could not be a den of iniquity or haven for criminals if the people
love Amen, Wisdom and Justice. If the people are righteous the government
will turn to righteousness; if the government is corrupt the people will turn to
corruption.

In this book is the wisdom of good governance by our ancestor handed down
through time, they ruled the longest, brightest, and greatest civilization on
earth known to man. To be Enderase Amen a "Noble Servant of God" is to
study the nobility of our progenitors; to learn it, to know it, to do it, and to
advance it.

Hotep, Ras Nahmir Amun

# Instruction of Rekhmire: Regulation laid on the Enderase Rekhmire

## THE TEACHING

1. His majesty said to him: Look to the office of Enderase, Watch over all that is done in it, Lo, it is the pillar for the whole land.

2. Lo, being Enderase, Lo, it is not sweet. Lo, it is bitter as gall. Lo, he is the copper that shields the gold of his masters house, Lo, he is not one who bends his face to magistrates and councilors, Not one who makes of anyone his client. Lo, what a man does in his master's house will be his happiness, Lo, he will not act of another.

3. Lo, petitioners come from the South and the North, The whole land is eager for [the counsel of the Enderase]; See to it that all is done according to law, That all is done exactly right, In his vindication. Lo, the magistrate who judges in public, Wind and water report all that he does, Lo, there is none who ignores his deeds. If he makes [a mistake in deciding] his case, And fails to reveal it through the mouth of the clerk, It will be known through the mouth of him whom he judged, Through his telling it to the clerk by saying: "This is not the decision of my case." If the petitioner is sent....or magistrate, One will not ignore what he did. Lo, the magistrate's safety is acting by the rule, In acting on a petitioner's speech; "I was not given my right."

4. Avoid what was said of the Enderase Akhtoy, That he denied his own people for the sake of others, For fear of being falsely called. If one of them appealed a judgment, that he had planned to do to him, He persisted in denying him, But that is excess of justice. Do not judge unfairly, Amen abhors partiality; This is an instruction, Plan to act accordingly. Regard one you know like one you don't know, One near you like one far from you. The magistrate who acts like this, He will succeed here in this place.

5. Do not pass over a petitioner, Before you have considered his speech. When a petitioner is about to petition you, Don't dismiss what he says as

already said. Deny him after you let him hear On what account you have denied him. Lo, it is said: "A petitioner wants his plea considered Rather than have his case adjudged." Do not scold a man wrongfully, Scold where scolding is due. Cast your fear, that you be feared, The feared magistrate is a magistrate. A magistrate's worth is that he does right, But if a man makes himself feared a million times, People think something is wrong with him, And they don't say of him, "He is a man."

6. This too is said: A magistrate who lies comes out as he deserves. Lo, you succeed in doing this office by doing justice, Lo, doing justice is what is wanted in the actions of the Enderase, Lo, the Enderase is its true guardian since the time of Amen. Lo, what one says of the Enderase's chief scribe: "Scribe of Justice" one says of him. As to the hall in which you judge, It has a room full of decisions. He who does justice before all people, He is the Enderase. Lo, a man remains in his office, If he acts as he is charged, Innocent is the man who acts as he is told. Do not act willfully In a case where the law is known; for as regards the headstrong man, The Lord prefers the timid to the headstrong man. Act then in accord with the charge given you. Lo.

**The Instruction of Hordedef**
**Son of Nesu Khufu 5th Dynasty Old Kingdom ca.2400 BCE**

## THE TEACHING

**1. He says: "Cleanse yourself before your own eyes, lest another cleanse You.**

2. When You prosper, found your household, take a mistress of heart, a son will be born to You. It is for the son that You build a house when You make a place for yourself. Make a good dwelling in the graveyard, make worthy your station in the Afterlife. Accept that death humbles us, accept that life exalts us, the house of death is for life. Seek for yourself well-watered fields.

### The Instruction to Kagemni
**Enderase of Nesu Snefru 6th Dynasty late Old Kingdom ca.2200 BCE**

---

## THE TEACHING

**1. The timid man prospers, praised is the fitting, open is the tent to the silent, spacious is the seat of the satisfied.**

2. Speak not too much! Sharp are the knives against he who transgresses the road, (he is) without speedy advance, except when he faults. When You sit with company, shun the food You like. Restraint of heart is only a brief moment! Gluttony is base and one points the finger at it. A cup of water quenches thirst, a mouthful of herbs strengthens the heart. A single good thing stands for goodness as a whole, a little something stands for much. Vile is he whose belly is voracious; time passes and he forgets in whose house the belly strides.

3. When You sit with a glutton, eat when his appetite has passed. When You drink with a drunkard, partake when his heart is happy. Do not grab your meat by the side of a glutton, (but) take when he gives You, do not refuse it, then it will soothe.

4. He who is blameless in matters of food, no word can prevail against him. The shy of face, even impassive of heart, the harsh is kinder to him than to his own mother, all people are his servants. Let your name go forth, while You are silent with your mouth. When You are summoned, be not great of heart, because of your strength among those your age, lest You be opposed. One knows not what may happen, and what Amen does when he punishes. The Enderase had his children summoned, after he had gained a complete knowledge of the ways of men, their character having come on him. In the end he said to them: 'All that is written in this book, heed it as I said it. Do not go beyond what has been set down.' Then they placed themselves on their bellies. They recited it aloud as it was written. It was good in their hearts beyond anything in this entire land. They stood and sat accordingly. Then the Majesty of King Huni of Upper and Lower Ta-Iterw died. The Majesty of King Snefru of Upper and Lower Ta-Iterw was raised up as beneficent King in this entire land. Kagemni was (then) made overseer of the city and Enderase. It is finished."

5

## The Instructions of PtahHotep
## 5th Dynasty Old Kingdom ca.3580 BCE

---

### THE DISCOURSE

1. Beginning of the maxims of good discourse, spoken by the prince, count, beloved, eldest son of the King, of his body, overseer of the city, Enderase Imhotep, teaching the ignorant in knowledge, and in the standard of good discourse, beneficial to him who hears, but woe to him who neglects them. So he spoke to his son:

2. "Don't let your heart get big because of your knowledge. Take counsel with the ignorant as well as with the scholar. For the limits of art are not brought, and no artisan is equipped with perfection. Good discourse is more hidden than green stone, yet may be found among the maids at the grindstones.

3. If You meet a disputant in his moment of action, one who directs his heart superior to You, fold your arms and bend your back. Do not seize your heart against him, for he will never agree with You. Belittle the evil speech, by not opposing him while he is in his moment. He will be called a know-nothing, when your control of heart will match his piles of words.

4. If You meet a disputant in his moment of action who is your equal, your peer, You will make your excellence exceed his by silence, even while he is speaking wrongly. There will be much talk among the hearers, and the knowledge the magistrates have of your name will be good.

5. If You meet a disputant in his moment of action, a man of little, not at all your equal, do not be aggressive of heart because he is weak, give him land for he will refute himself. Do not answer him to relieve your heart. Do not wash the heart against your opponent. Wretched is he who injures a man of little heart. One will wish to do what your heart desires. You will strike him with the reproof of the magistrates.

6. If You are a man who leads, charged to direct the affairs of a great number, seek out every well-adjusted deed, so that your conduct may be blameless. Great is Ma'at, lasting in effect. Undisturbed since the time of Ausar. One punishes the transgressor of laws, though the heart that robs overlooks this.

Baseness may seize riches, yet crime never lands its wares. He says: 'I acquire for myself.' He does not say: 'I acquire for my function.' In the end, it is Ma'at that lasts, (and) man says: 'It is my father's domain.'

7. Do not scheme against people, for Amen punishes accordingly. If a man nevertheless says: 'I will live that way.', he will lack bread for his mouth. If a man says: 'I will be rich.' He will have to say: 'My cleverness has snared me.' If a man says: 'I will rob someone.', he will, in the end, make a gift to a stranger! People's schemes do not prevail. Amen's command is what prevails. Live then in the midst of peace with what You have, for what Amen gives comes by itself.

8. If You get to be among guests, at the dining table of one greater than You, accept what he gives, in the way it is set before your nose. Look at what is before You, do not pierce it with lots of glances: it offends the Ka to be molested. Do not speak until he summons, since one does not know whether he has evil on his heart. Speak when he addresses You, and may your words please the heart. The nobleman, sitting behind the breads, behaves as his Ka commands him. He will give to him whom he favors, for that is the custom when the night has come. It is the Ka that makes his hands reach out. The great man gives to the lucky man. So the breads are eaten under the plan of Amen, a fool is who complains of it.

9. If You are a man of trust, sent by one great man to another, be exact when he sends You.

10. Give his message as he said it. Guard against slanderous speech, which embroils one great with another. Keep to Ma'at, do not exceed it. But the washing of the heart should not be repeated. Do not speak against anyone, great or small, the Ka abhors it.

11. If You plow and there is growth in the field, because Amen lets it prosper in your hand, do not boast about it at your neighbor's side, for one has great respect for the silent man. If a man of good character is a man of wealth, he takes possession like a crocodile, even in court. Do not impose on one who is childless: neither criticize, nor boast of it.

7

12. There is many a father who has grief, and a mother of children less content than another without. It is the lonely whom Amen fosters, while the family man prays for a follower.

13. If You are a weakling, serve a man of quality, worthy of trust, so that all your conduct may be well with Amen. Do not recall if once he was of humble condition, do not let your heart become big toward him, for knowing his former state. Respect him for what has accrued to him, for surely goods do not come by themselves. There are laws for him whom the Neter love. His gain, he gathered it himself, but it is Amen who makes him worthy, and protects him while he sleeps.

14. Follow your heart as long as You live. Do no more than is required. Do not shorten the time of 'follow-the-heart', for trimming its moment offends the Ka. Do not waste time on daily cares beyond providing for your household. When wealth has come, follow your heart! Wealth does no good if one is annoyed!

15. If You are a man of quality, worthy of trust, may You produce a son, by the favor of Amen. If he is straight, turns around your character, takes care of your possessions in good order, then accomplish for him all that is good. He is your son, belonging to the seed of your Ka, so do not withdraw your heart from him. But an offspring can make trouble; if he goes into the wrong direction, neglects your counsel, with insolence disobeys all that is said, if his mouth sprouts evil speech, then put him to work for the totality of his talk! They disfavor him who crosses You, for his obstacle was fated in the womb. He whom they guide cannot go astray, but whom they make boatless cannot cross.

16. If You are in a court of justice, stand or sit as fits your rank, assigned to You on the first day. Do not force your way in, for You will be turned back. Keen is the face of him who enters announced, spacious in the court of justice has a correct method, all behavior is by the plumb-line. It is Amen who gives the seat. He who uses elbows is not helped.

17. If You are among the people, gain allies through being trustful of heart. The trustful of heart does not vent his belly's speech. He will himself become a man, who commands, a man of means thanks to his behavior. May your name be good without You talking about it. Your body is sleek; your face turns towards your people, and one praises You without You knowing it. (But) him whose heart obeys his belly disappears; he raises contempt of himself in place of love. His heart is denuded, his body un-anointed. The great of heart is a gift of Amen. He who obeys his belly, obeys the enemy.

18. Report your commission without swallowing the heart, and give your advice in your master's council. If he is fluent in his speech, it will not be hard for the envoy to report, nor will he be answered: 'Who is he to know it?' As to the master, his affairs will fail, if he plans to punish him for it. He should be silent and conclude: 'I have spoken.' By the seat of him who has been called.

19. If You are a man who leads, that your way to govern may freely travel. You should do outstanding things. Remember the day that comes after, (so that) no strife will occur in the midst of honors. (Indeed), where a hiding crocodile emerges, hatred arises.

20. If You are a man who leads, calmly hear the speech of one who pleads, (and) do not stop him from purging his body of that which he planned to tell. A man in distress wants to wish his heart more than that his case be won. About him who stops a plea, one says: 'Why does he reject it?' Not all one pleads for can be granted, but a good hearing calms the heart.

21. If You want friendship to endure in the house You enter, as master, brother, or friend, or in whatever place You enter, beware of approaching the women! Unhappy is the place where it is done. Their face is not keen on he who intrudes on them. A thousand men are turned away from their good. In a short moment like a dream, then death comes for having known them. Poor advice is 'shoot the opponent'! When one goes to do it, the heart rejects it. (But) as for him who fails through lust of them, no affair of his can prosper.

22. If You want your conduct to be perfect, deliver yourself from every evil, and combat against the greed of the heart. It is a grievous sickness without

9

cure, impossible to penetrate. It causes disaster among fathers and mothers, among the brothers of the mother, and parts wife from husband. It is an amalgam of all evils, a bundle of all hateful things. That man endures who correctly applies Ma'at, and walks according to his stride. He will make a will by it. The greed of the heart has no tomb!

23. Do not be greedy of heart in the division of goods. Do not covet more than your share. Do not be greedy of heart toward your kin. The kind has a greater claim than the rude. The family of the latter reveals very little, for he is deprived of what speech brings. Even a little of what is craved, makes conflict rise in a cool-bellied man.

24. When you prosper, found your house, Love your wife with ardor, Fill her belly; clothe her back, Ointment is a remedy for her body. Gladden her heart as long as you live. She is a fertile field, useful to her husband. Do not contend with her in a court of justice, Keep her from the powers; restrain her from it. For her eye is her storm when she gazes. You will make her peaceful in your house. If you push her back, see the tears! Her vagina is one of her forms of action. What she enforces, is that a canal be made for her.

25. Satisfy those who enter, and in whom You trust, with what You make, for You make it by the favor of Amen. Of him who fails to satisfy those who enter, and in whom he trusts, one says: 'A Ka too pleased with itself!'. What will come is unknown, even if one understands tomorrow. The proper Ka is a correct Ka at peace with itself.

26. If praiseworthy deeds are done, trustworthy friends will say: 'Welcome!' One does not bring supplies to town, one brings friends when there is need.

27. Do not repeat gossip, neither hear it. It is the way of expression of the hot-bellied. Report a thing observed, not heard. If it is negligible, do not say anything, and see: he who is before You recognizes your worth. Let it be ordered to seize what it produces. In accordance with the law, hatred will arise against him who seizes it to use it. Gossip is like a vision against which one covers the face.

28. If You are a man of quality, worthy of trust, who sits in his master's council, bring your whole heart together towards excellence. Your silence is more useful than chatter. Speak when You know how to untie the knot. It is the skilled who speak in council. Speaking is harder than all other work. He who unties it makes it serve.

29. If You are mighty, gain respect through knowledge and gentleness of speech. Do not command except as is fitting. He who provokes gets into trouble. Do not be high of heart, lest You be humbled. Do not be mute, lest You be reprimanded. When You answer one who is fuming, avert your face, control yourself, or the flames of the hot of heart sweep across. He who steps gently finds his path paved. All day long the sad of heart has no happy moment. All day long the frivolous of heart cannot keep house. The archers complete the aim, as one who holds the rudder until it touches land. The opposing is imprisoned. He who obeys his heart is equipped to order.

30. Do not oppose a great man's action. Do not vex the heart of one who is burdened. His anger manifests against him who combats him. The Ka of the great one will part from him who loves him. Yet he who provides is together with Amen. What he wishes will be done for him. When he turns his face back to You after raging, then there will be peace from his Ka, and hostility from the enemy. To provide increases love.

31. Teach the great what is useful to him, be his aid before the people. Let his knowledge fall back on his master, and your sustenance will come from his Ka. As the favorite's belly is filled, so your back is clothed by it, and his help will be there to sustain You. For your superior whom You love, and who lives by it, he in turn will give You good support. So will love of You endure, in the belly of those who love You. Behold: it is the Ka that loves to listen.

32. If You are a magistrate of standing, commissioned to appease the many, remove stupidity from the record. When You speak, do not lean to one side, beware lest one complain: 'Judges, he puts his speech on the side he likes!' In court, your deeds will then turn against You.

33. If You are angered by a misdeed, then lean toward the man only on account of his rectitude. Pass over the old error, do not recall it, since he was silent to You on the first day.

11

34. If You are great after having been humble, have gained wealth after having been poor in the past, in a town which You know, then knowing your former condition, do not put the trust of your heart in your heaps, which came to You as gifts of Amen, so that You will not fall behind one like You, to whom the same has happened.

35. Bend your back to your superior, your overseer from the palace, then your house will endure in its wealth, and your rewards will be in their right place. Wretched is he who opposes a superior, for one lives as long as he is mild...Baring the arm does not hurt it! Do not plunder a neighbor's house, and do not steal the goods of one near You, so that he does not denounce You, before You are heard. A quarreler lacks in heart, so if he is known as an aggressor, the hostile will have trouble in the neighborhood.

36. Do not copulate with an angry woman, for You know that one will fight against the water on her heart. What is in her belly will not be refreshed. That during the night she does not do what is repelled, but be calmed after having ended the offense of her heart.

37. If You seek to probe the true nature of a friend, do not inquire after him, but approach him yourself. Then deal with him alone, until You are no longer uncertain about his condition.

38. After a time, dispute with him. Test his heart in dialogue. If what he has seen of himself escapes him, if he does a thing that irritates You, be yet friendly with him or be silent, but do not turn away your face. Restrain yourself and open dialogue. Do not answer with an act of hostility. Neither counter him, nor humiliate him. His time does not fail to come...for one does not escape what is fated.

39. Be bright-faced as long as You exist! But what leaves the storehouse does not return. It is the food to be distributed which is coveted. But one whose belly is empty is an accuser, and one deprived becomes an opponent. Do not have him for a neighbor. Kindness is a man's memorial; for the years after his function.

40. Know those at your side, and then your goods endure. Do not be weak of character toward your friends, they are a riverbank to be turned and filled more important than its riches...For what belongs to one also belongs to another! The good deed profits the son-of-man. An accomplished nature is a memorial.

41.Punish as a commander-in-chief, but teach the complete form! The act of stopping crime is an enduring good example. Crime, except for misfortune, turns the complainer into an aggressor.

42. If You take to wife a woman of good quality, who is unbound of heart and known by her town, conform her to the double law. Be pleasant to her when the moment is right, do not separate yourself from her and let her eat, for the joyful of heart confer an exact balance."

**On Hearing & Listening**

43. "If You hear my sayings, all your plans will go forward. In their act of Ma'at lies their value. Their memory lingers on in the speech of men, because of the accomplishment of their command! If every word is carried on, they will not perish in this land. That an advice be given for the good, so that the great will speak accordingly. It is teaching a man to speak to what comes after him. He who hears this becomes a master-hearer. It is good to speak to posterity, it will hear it. If a good example is set by him who leads, he will be beneficent forever, and his wisdom will be for all time. He who knows, feeds his Ba with what endures, so that it is happy with him on Earth. He who knows is known by his wisdom, and the great by his good actions. That his heart twines his tongue, and his lips be precise when he speaks. That his eyes see! That his ears be pleased to hear what profits his son. For acting with Ma'at, he is free of falsehood. Useful is listening to a son who hears! If hearing enters the hearer, the hearer becomes a listener. To listen well is to speak well. He who listens is a master of what is good. Splendid is listening to one who hears! Listening is better than all else. It manifests perfect love. How good it is for a son to grasp his father's words? Underneath them, he will reach old age.

## On the Listener and the Non-Listener

44. He who listens is beloved of Amen, he who does not listen is shunned by Amen. It is the heart, which makes of its owner a listener or a non-listener. Life, prosperity & health are a man's heart. It is the hearer who listens to what is said. He who loves to listen, is one who does what is said. How good for a son to obey his father!

45. How happy is he the son to whom it is said: 'The son pleases as a master of listening.' He the son who hears the one the father who said this is well adjusted in his inner being, and honored by his father. His remembrance is in the mouth of the living, those on Earth and those who will be. If the son-of-man accepts his father's words, no plan of his will go wrong. Teach your son to be a hearer, one who will be valued by the heart of the nobles, one who guides his mouth by what he was told, one regarded as a listener. This son excels, his deeds stand out, while failure enters him who listens not. The knower wakes early to his lasting form, while the fool is hard pressed. The fool who does not listen, can accomplish nothing at all. He sees knowledge as ignorance, usefulness as harmfulness. He does all that is detestable, and is blamed for it each day. He lives on that by which one dies, he feeds on damned speech. His sort is known to the officials, to wit: 'A living death each day!' One passes over his doings, because of his many daily troubles. A son who listens, is a Follower of Heru. It goes well with him when he listens.

46. When he is old and reaches veneration, may he speak likewise to his children, renewing the teaching of his father. Every man teaches as he acts. May he speak to the children, so that they may speak to their children. Set an example, do not give offense. If Ma'at stands firm, your children live! As to the first who comes as a carrier of evil, may people say to what they see: 'That is then just like him!' And may they say to what they hear: 'That is then just like him!' Let everyone see them the children to appease the multitudes. Without them, riches are useless.

14

## On Speaking

47. Do not talk a word and then bring it back. Do not put one thing in place of another. Beware of loosening the cords in You, lest a man of knowledge say: 'Hear! If You want to endure in the mouth of the listeners, speak only after You have mastered the craft!'. If You speak in a refined way, all your plans will be in place. Immerse your heart, control your mouth, then You are known among the officials.

48. Be quite exact before your master, act so that he says: 'He is a son !' And those who hear it will say: 'Blessed is he to whom he was born!'. Be patient of heart the moment You speak, so as to say elevated things. In this way, the nobles who hear it will say: 'How good is what comes from his mouth!' Act so that your master will say of You: 'How accomplished is he whom his father taught. When he came forth from him, issued from his body, he the father spoke to him when he was in the belly of his mother, and he the son accomplished even more than he was told.' Lo, the good son, the gift of Amen, exceeds what is told to him by his master, he does Ma'at and his heart matches his steps. O my son as You succeed me, with a sound body, the King at peace with all what is done, may You obtain many years of life!

## Concluding Remarks

49. Not small is what I did on Earth...I had hundred and ten years of life, as a gift of the King, and honors exceeding those of the ancestors. For by doing Ma'at for the King, the venerated place comes." From its beginning to its end, in accordance with how it was found in writing.

**The Instruction to Merikare**
King Khety to his son  Merikare-
11th Dynasty First Intermediary Period ca.2134 BCE

___

THE TEACHING

## On Rebellion

1. May You be justified before Amen, that a man may say even in your absence that You punish in accordance with the offense!

2. A good character is a man's heaven, but the cursing of the furious of heart is painful. If You are skilled in speech, You will win. The tongue is the sword of the King.

3. Speaking is stronger than any weapon. No one can overcome the skillful heart. Teach your people on the mat, the wise is a school to the officials. Those who know that he knows will not attack him, no misfortune occurs when he is near. Justice or truth comes to him distilled, like the intentions of the sayings of the ancestors.

## Dealing with Officials and Commoners

4. Copy your fathers, your  ancestors, work is done successfully with their knowledge. Look, their words endure in writings! Open, read and copy their knowledge! He who is taught becomes skilled. Do not be evil, kindness of heart is good. Let your memorial last through love of You. Increase the hired-workers; befriend the town-folk, and Amen will be praised for the donations, one will watch over your reputation praise your goodness, and pray for your health. Respect the officials, sustain your people, strengthen your borders, your frontier patrols. It is good to work for the future! One respects the life of the foresighted, while the trustful heart fails. Make people come to You through your good nature. A wretch is who desires the land of his neighbors.

5. A fool is who covets what others possess. Life on Earth passes; it is not long. Happy is he who is remembered. A million men do not benefit the Lord of the Two Lands. Is there a man who lives forever? He who comes with Ausar passes by, just as he leaves who indulged himself. Make your officials King who has councilors. Wealthy is he who is rich in his officials. Speak truth in your house, that the officials of the land may respect You. Righteousness of heart is proper for the Lord (of the Two Lands). The front of the house puts awe in the back. Do justice, then You endure on Earth. Calm the weeper, do not oppress the widow, do not expel a man from his father's property, do not reduce the officials in their possessions. Beware of punishing wrongfully. Do not kill, it does not serve You. Punish with beatings, with detention, so will the land be well-ordered. Except for the rebel, whose plans are found out, for Karma knows the malcontent of heart. Great, so that they act by your laws. He who has wealth at home will not be partial, for he is a rich man who lacks nothing. The poor man does not speak justly. One who says: 'I wish I had." is unrighteous, for he inclines to him who will pay him. Great is the man whose great men are great. Strong is the The Neter smites the rebels in blood. He who is merciful will increase his lifetime. Do not kill a man whose excellence You know, with whom You used to chant the writings, who was brought up and recognized before Amen, with free striding feet in the place of secrets! The *Ba* comes to the place it knows, it does not miss its former path, no kind of science holds it back, it comes to those who give it water. The court that judges the needy, You know they are not lenient, on the day of judging the miserable, in the hour of doing their task! It is painful when the accuser has knowledge...Let your heart not trust in length of years, for they review a lifetime in an hour! When, after death, a man remains over, his deeds are set beside him in a heap, and being there lasts forever! A fool is who does what they reprove! He who reaches them without having done wrong, will exist there like a Neter, free-striding like the Lords of Eternity!

**Advice on Raising Troops and Religious Duties**

6. Raise your young soldiers and the residence will love You. Increase your supporters among the helpers. See, your town is full of new growth. These twenty years, the youth has been happy, following its heart. The helpers are now going forth once again, veterans return to their children. I raised troops from on my accession. Make your great ones great, and promote your

17

soldiers. Increase the youth of your following, equip with amounts, endow with fields, reward them with herds. Do not prefer the well born to the commoner, but choose a man on account of his skills, then every work of craft will be done! Guard your borders, secure your forts, troops are useful to their Lord. Make many monuments to Amen, this keeps alive their maker's name. A man should do what profits his *Ba*: perform the monthly service, wear the white sandals, visit the temple, be discreet concerning the secrets, enter the shrine, eat bread in the house of Amen, pour libations, multiply the loaves, make ample the daily offerings. It is good for him who does it. Endow your monuments according to your wealth. Even one day gives to eternity, and an hour contributes to the future. The servant knows the Master he works for, even when your statues are brought to far foreign countries, who do not give tribute.

**The Historical Section**

7. Diseased and deprived is he who imprisons the evil gang of rebels, for the enemy cannot be calm within Ta-Iterw. Troops will fight troops, as the ancestors foretold. Ta-Iterw fought in the necropolis, destroying tombs in vengeful destruction. I did the like, and the like happened, as is done to one who strays from the path of Ma'at...Do not deal evilly with the Southland, You know what the residence foretold about it. As this happened so that may happen. But they have not transgressed like they said! I attacked Thinis and Maki, opposite its southern border at Tawet. I engulfed it like a flood! King Mer ib re, the justified, had not done this, so be merciful on account of this {to the encumbered}. Make peace, renew the treaties. No river lets itself be hidden. It is good to work for the future. You stand well with the Southland, they come to You bearing tribute, with gifts. I have acted like the forefathers; if one has no grain to give, be kind, since they are humble before You. Be sated with your bread, your beer...Granite comes to You unhindered. Do not despoil the monuments of another, but quarry stone in Tura.

8. Do not build your tomb out of ruins, using what had been made for what is to be made. Behold, the King is the Lord of Joy! May You rest, sleep in your strength, follow your heart, through what I have done: there is no foe within your borders. I arose as Lord of the City, whose heart was sad because of the Northland. From Hetshenu to {Sembaqa, and its southern border at Two-Fish

18

Channel.} I pacified the entire West as far as the coast of the Lake. It pays taxes, it gives cedar wood. One sees juniper wood which they give us. The East abounds in bowmen, and their labor does arrive. The middle islands are turned back, and every man from amongst them. The temples say: 'You are greater than I!'. Look, the land they had ravaged has been made into nomes, (and) all kinds of large towns {are in it}. What was ruled by one is in the hands of ten, officials are appointed, and tax-lists drawn up. When free men are given land, they work for You like a single team. No rebellious heart will arise among them, and Happiness will not fail to come. The dues of the North lands are in your hand, for the mooring-post is staked in the district I made in the East, from Hebenu to The Ways of Heru. It is settled with towns, filled with people, of the best in the whole land, to repel attacks against them.

9. May I see a brave man who will do the like, who will add to what I have done. For a vile heir would disgrace me. But this should be said to the bowmen: "The miserable Asiatic, is wretched because of the place he is in; short of water, bare of wood, its paths are many and painful because of mountains. He does not dwell in one place, and food propels his legs. He fights since the time of Heru, not conquering nor being conquered, he does not announce the day of combat, like a thief who hides for a (united) group." But as I live and will be what I am, these bowmen were a sealed wall. I breached {their strongholds}, I made Lower Ta-Iterw attack them, I captured their inhabitants, I seized their cattle, until the Asiatics abhorred Ta-Iterw. Do not concern yourself with him, for the Asiatic is a crocodile on its shore; it snatches from a lonely road, but it cannot seize from a populous town! Medenyt has been restored to its Nome, its one side is irrigated as far as Kem-Wer. It is the defense against the bowmen. Its walls are warlike, its soldiers many, its farmers know how to bear arms, apart from the free men within.

10. The region of Ineb Hedj totals ten thousand men, free citizens who are not taxed. Officials are in it since the time it was residence, the borders are firm, the garrisons valiant. Many northerners irrigate it as far as the Northland, taxed with grain in the manner of free men. For those who do this, this is the way to surpass me. Look, it is the gateway of the Northland! It has acted as a dike as far as Hwt-nen-nesu! Abundant citizens are the support of the heart. Beware of being surrounded by the soldiers of the foe. Caution

prolongs life. If your southern border is attacked, it means the bowmen of Ta Seti have put on the war belt! Build buildings in the Northland! As the name of a man is not made small by his actions, so a settled town is not harmed. Build a temple for your statue. The foe loves grieving the heart and vile deeds.

## The Glory of Kingship

10. King Khety, the justified, laid down in teaching: "He who is silent of heart towards violence diminishes the land. Do not say: "It is weakness of heart!", and do not slacken your actions. He who opposes You disturbs the sky. The monuments are sound for a hundred years. If the foe understood this, he would not attack them. But there is no one who has no enemy.
The Lord of the Two Shores is one who knows, and the King, the Lord of Courtiers, is not foolish, for as one who is wise did he come from the womb? From a million men, the Neter singled him out...A goodly office is kingship, it has no son, no brother to maintain its memorial. But one man provides for the other: a man acts for him who was before him, so that what he has done is preserved by his successor. Look, a shameful deed occurred in my time; the Nome of Thinis was ravaged! Though it happened through my doing, I learned it after it was done. There was retribution for what I had done. For it is evil to destroy, useless to restore what one has damaged, or to rebuild what one has demolished. Beware of it! With its like, a blow is repaid, and to every action there is a response.

## Divine Justice

11. Generation succeeds generation, while Amen, who knows their characters, has hidden Himself. One cannot resist the Lord of the Hand, for He reaches all that the eyes can see...One should revere Amen on his path, made of costly stones, fashioned of bronze. As watercourse is replaced by watercourse, so no river allows itself to be concealed, and it breaks the channel in which it was hidden. So also, the Ba goes to the place it knows, and strays not from its former path. Make worthy your house of the Afterlife, make firm your station in the afterlife, by being upright, by doing justice, on which the hearts of men rely. The loaf of the upright is preferred to the ox of the evildoer. Work for Amen, Amen will also work for You; with offerings that make the altar flourish, with cravings that proclaim your name. Amen thinks of him who works for Him!

**Hymn to the Creator Amen**

12. Well-tended is humanity - the cattle of Amen: he made sky and Earth for their sake, he subdued the water monster, he made breath for their noses to live. They are his images, who came from his body. He shines in the sky for their sake. He made for them plants and cattle, fowl and fish to feed them. He slew his foes, reduced his children, when they thought of making rebellion. He makes daylight for their sake, he sails by to see them. He has built his shrine around them, when they weep he hears. He made for them rulers in the egg, leaders to raise the back of the weak. He made for them science as weapons, to ward off the blow of events, watching over them by day and by night. He has punished the traitors among them, as a man punishes his son for the sake of his house. For Amen knows every name.

**Epilogue**

13. Do no ill against my speech, which lays down all the laws of kingship, which instructs You, that You may rule the land! And may You reach me with none to accuse You! Do not kill one who is close to You, whom You have favored, Amen knows him. He is one of the fortunate ones on Earth...
for divine are they who follow the King! Make yourself loved by everyone, for a good character is remembered. When time has passed, may You be called: 'He who ended the time of trouble by those who come after the House of Khety, in thinking of what has come today. Look, I have told You the best of my thoughts! Act by what is set before You!"

## The Instruction of Amenemat
**To his son Nesu Senusret I 12th Dynasty - Middle Kingdom ca.1909 BCE**

---

## PROLOGUE
Beginning of the instruction made by the Majesty of King Sehetepibre, son of Re, Amenemhat, the justified, as he spoke in a mission of truth, to his son the All-Lord.

### THE TEACHING

### Address to Senusret

**1. He said: "Risen as a Neter, hear what I tell You, so that You may rule the land, govern the shores, and increase well-being!**

### Beware of Nobodies
2. Beware of subjects, who are nobodies, of whose plotting one is not aware. Do not go near them alone. Trust not a brother, no, not a friend, make no intimates, it is worthless. When You lie down, guard your heart yourself. For no man has an adherent on the day of woe.

### By Doing Good One does not Avoid an Attack
3. I gave to the beggar, I raised the orphan, I gave to those who were nothing, like to those who were something. But he who ate my food raised opposition, he whom I gave my hands, used them to assail me, wearers of my fine linen looked at me as if they were needy, those perfumed with my myrrh {poured water while wearing it.}

### Remember What has Happened
4. You my living peers, my partners among men, make for me mourning such as has not been heard, for so great a combat had not yet been seen! If one fights in the arena forgetful of the past, success will elude him who ignores what he should know.

### The Narrative of the Assassination
5. It was after supper, night had come. I was taking an hour of rest, lying on

my bed, for I was weary. As my heart began to follow sleep, weapons for my protection were turned against me, while I was like a snake of the desert. I awoke at the fighting, {came to myself}, and found it was a combat of the guard. Had I quickly seized weapons in my hand, I would have made the cowards retreat. But no one is strong at night; no one can fight alone; no success is achieved without a helper.

6. So bloodshed occurred while I was without You; before the courtiers had heard I would hand over to You; before I had sat with You so as to advise You. For I had not prepared for it, had not expected it, had not foreseen the failing of the servants the exceptional nature of this murder. Had women (of the harem) ever marshaled troops? Are rebels nurtured inside the palace? {Or did destroyers break into the place?} {(It is) a bad memory because of what these miserable people did.} No harm had come to me since my birth, (and) no one equaled me as a doer of deeds.

### The Confession of Excellence
7. I journeyed to Yebu, I returned to the Delta. Having stood on the land's borders, I observed its interior. I reached the borders of the strongholds; by my strength and my being. I was grain-maker, beloved of Nepri. Hapy honored me on every field. None hungered in my years. None thirsted in them. One sat because I acted and spoke of myself; I had assigned everything to its place. I subdued lions, I captured crocodiles, I repressed those of Wawat, I captured the Medjay, I made the Asiatics do the dog walk.

### Preparing His Son
8. I built myself a house decked with gold, its ceiling of lapis lazuli, walls of silver, floors of [acacia wood], doors of copper, bolts of bronze. The serfs (however) plotted against me. Be prepared against this! If You know this, then You are its Lord, You the All-Lord. Behold, much hatred is in the streets. The wise says 'yes', the fool says 'no' for he has not understood it, as his face is lacking eyes, (that You) were my own tongue, Senusret my son, when I (still) walked on my feet, (that You) were my own heart, when my eyes still saw You, the child of a happy hour.

## Concluding Advise

9. See, I made the beginning, You will tie the end. I have landed by the dead, (and) You wear the White Crown of Amen's son. The seal is in its correct place, (and) jubilation has started for You in the bark of Ra Ascend to the throne for a government better than most, not like mine! Be courageous, raise your monuments, establish your strongholds, and beware of those You know, for I do not wish them on the side of your Majesty."

The Instruction of Amenemope

## Chapter 1

**1. Give your ears and hear what is said, Give your mind over to their
interpretation: It is profitable to put them in your heart, But woe to him
that neglects them! Let them rest in the shrine of your insides. That they
may act as a lock in your heart; Now when there comes a storm of words,
They will be a mooring post on your tongue.**

2. If you spend a lifetime with these things in your heart, You will find it good
fortune; You will discover my words to be a treasure house of life,
And your body will flourish on earth.

## Chapter 2

3. Beware of stealing from a miserable man and of raging against the cripple.
Do not stretch out your hand to touch an old man, nor snip at the words of an
elder. Don't let yourself be involved in a fraudulent business, nor desire the
carrying out of it; Do not get tired because of being interfered with, nor return
an answer on your own. The evildoer, throw him <in> the canal,
And he will bring back its slime. The north wind comes down and ends his
appointed hour, It is joined to the tempest; The thunder is high, the crocodiles
are nasty, 'O hot-headed man, what are you like?' he cries out, and his voice
(reaches) heaven. O Moon, make his crime manifest! Row that we may ferry
the evil man away, For we will not act according to his evil nature; Lift him
up, give him your hand, And leave him in the hands of Amen; Fill his gut
with your own food That he may be sated and ashamed. Something else of
value in the heart of Amen Is to stop and think before speaking.

## Chapter 3

4. Do not get into a quarrel with the argumentative man nor incite him with
words; Proceed cautiously before an opponent, And give way to an
adversary; Sleep on it before speaking, For a storm come forth like fire in hay
is The hot-headed man in his appointed time. May you be restrained before
him; Leave him to himself, And Amen will know how to answer him. If you
spend your life with these things in your heart, Your children will see them.

## Chapter 4

5. The hot-headed man in the temple is like a tree grown indoors; Only for a moment does it put forth roots. It reaches its end in the carpentry shop, It is floated away far from its place, Or fire is its funeral pyre. The truly temperate man sets himself apart, he is like a tree grown in a sunlit field, But it flourishes, it doubles its yield, It stands before its owner; Its fruit is something sweet, its shade is pleasant, And it reaches its end as a statue.

## Chapter 5

6. Do not take by violence the shares of the temple, Do not be grasping, and you will find overabundance; Do not take away a temple servant In order to acquire the property of another man. Do not say today is the same as tomorrow, Or how will matters come to pass? When tomorrow comes, today is past; The deep waters sink from the canal bank, Crocodiles are uncovered, the hippopotamuses are on dry land, And the fishes gasping for air; The wolves are fat, the wild fowl in festival, And the nets are drained.

7. Every temperate man in the temple says, "Great is the benevolence of Ra." Fill yourself with silence, you will find life, And your body will flourish on earth.

## Chapter 6

8. Do not displace the surveyor's marker on the boundaries of the arable land, Nor alter the position of the measuring line; Do not be greedy for a plot of land, Nor overturn the boundaries of a widow. As for the road in the field worn down by time, He who takes it violently for fields, If he traps by deceptive attestations, Will be lassoed by the might of the moon.

9. To one who has done this on earth, pay attention, For he is a weak enemy; He is an enemy overturned inside himself; Life is taken from his eye; His household is hostile to the community, His storerooms are toppled over, His property taken from his children, And to someone else his possessions given.

10. Take care not to topple over the boundary marks of the arable land, Not fearing that you will be brought to court; Man appeases Amen by the might of the Lord When he sets straight the boundaries of the arable land.

11. Desire, then, to make yourself prosper, And take care for the Lord of All; Do not trample on the furrow of someone else, Their good order will be profitable for you.

12. So plough the fields, and you will find whatever you need, And receive the bread from your own threshing floor: Better is the bushel which Amen gives you Than five thousand deceitfully gotten; They do not spend a day in the storehouse or warehouse, They are no use for dough for beer; Their stay in the granary is short-lived, When morning comes they will be swept away. Better, then, is poverty in the hand of Amen Than riches in the storehouse; Better is bread when the mind is at ease Than riches with anxiety.

## Chapter 7

13. Do not set your heart on seeking riches, For there is no one who can ignore Destiny and Fortune; Do not set your thoughts on external matters; For every man there is his appointed time.

14. Do not exert yourself to seek out excess And your wealth will prosper for you; If riches come to you by theft They will not spend the night with you; As soon as day breaks they will not be in your household; Although their places can be seen, they are not there.

15. When the earth opens up its mouth, it levels him and swallows him up, And it drowns him in the deep; They have made for themselves a great hole which suites them. And they have sunk themselves in the tomb; Or they have made themselves wings like geese, And they fly up to the sky. Do not be pleased with yourself (because of) riches acquired through robbery, Neither complain about poverty. If an officer commands one who goes in front of him, His company leaves him; The boat of the covetous is abandoned <in> the mud, While the skiff of the truly temperate man sails on. When he rises you will meditate on Amun, Saying, "Grant me prosperity and health." And he will give you your necessities for life, And you will be safe from fear.

## Chapter 8

16. Set your good deeds throughout the world That you may greet everyone; They make rejoicing for the Wisdom, And spit against the Evil. Keep your tongue safe from words of detraction, And you will be the loved one of the people, Then you will find your place within the temple And your offerings among the bread deliveries of your lord; You will be revered, when you are concealed in your grave, And be safe from the might of Amen.

17. Do not accuse a man, When the news of an escape is concealed. If you hear something good or bad, Say it outside, where it is not heard; Set a good report on your tongue, While the bad thing is covered up inside you.

## Chapter 9

18. Do not fraternize with the hot-tempered man, Nor approach him to converse. Safeguard your tongue from answering your superior, And take care not to speak against him. Do not allow him to cast words only to entrap you, And be not too free in your reply; With a man of your own station discuss the reply; And take care of speaking thoughtlessly; When a man's heart is upset, words travel faster Than wind and rain. He is ruined and created by his tongue, And yet he speaks slander; He makes an answer deserving of a beating, For its work is evil; He sails among all the world, But his cargo is false words; He acts the ferryman in knitting words; He goes forth and comes back arguing.

19. But whether he eats or whether he drinks inside, His accusation (waits for him) without. The day when his evil deed is brought to court Is a disaster for his children. He is like a wolf cub in the farmyard, And he turns one eye to the other (squinting), For he sets families to argue. He goes before all the wind like clouds, He darkens his color in the sun; He crocks his tail like a baby crocodile, He curls himself up to inflict harm, His lips are sweet, but his tongue is bitter, And fire burns inside him.

20. Do not fly up to join that man Not fearing you will be brought to account.

## Chapter 10

21. Do not address your intemperate friend in your unrighteousness, Nor destroy your own mind; Do not say to him, "May you be praised", not meaning it When there is fear within you. Do not converse falsely with a man, For it is the abomination of Amen. Do not separate your mind from your tongue, All your plans will succeed. You will be important before others, While you will be secure in the hand of Amen.

22. Amen hates one who falsified words, His great abomination is duplicity.

## Chapter 11

23. Do not covet the property of the dependent Nor hunger for his bread; The property of a dependent blocks the throat, It is vomit for the gullet. If he has engendered it by false oaths, His heart slips back inside him. It is through the disaffected that success is lost, Bad and good elude.

24. If you are at a loss before your superior, And are confused in your speeches, Your flattering are turned back with curses, And your humble action by beatings. Whoever fills the mouth with too much bread swallows it and spits up, So he is emptied of his good.

25. To the examination of a dependant give thought While the sticks touch him, And while all his people are fettered with manacles: Who is to have the execution? When you are too free before your superior, Then you are in bad favor with your subordinates, So steer away from the poor man on the road, That you may see him but keep clear of his property.

## Chapter 12

26. Do not covet the property of an official, And do not fill your mouth with too much food extravagantly; If he sets you to manage his property, Respect his, and yours will prosper.

27. Do not deal with the intemperate man, Nor associate yourself to a disloyal party.

28. If you are sent to transport straw, Respect its account; If a man is detected in a dishonest transaction, Never again will he be employed.

## Chapter 13

29. Do not lead a man astray with reed pen or papyrus document; It is the abomination of Amen. Do not witness a false statement, Nor remove a man from the list by your order; Do not enroll someone who has nothing, Nor make your pen be false. If you find a large debt against a poor man, Make it into three parts; Release two of them and let one remain; You will find it a path of life; You will pass the night in sound sleep; in the morning You will find it like good news.

30. Better it is to be praised as one loved by men Than wealth in the storehouse; Better is bread when the mind is at ease Than riches with troubles.

## Chapter 14

31. Do not pay attention to a person, Nor exert yourself to seek out his hand, If he says to you, "take a bribe," It is not an insignificant matter to be cautious of him; Do not avert your glance from him, nor bend down your head, Nor turn aside your gaze. Address him with your words and say to him greetings; When he stops, your chance will come; Do not repel him at his first approach, Another time he will be brought to judgment.

## Chapter 15

32. Do well, and you will attain influence. Do not dip your reed against the one who sins. The beak of the Ibis is the finger of the scribe; Take care not to disturb it; Tehuti rests in the temple of Khmun, While his eye travels around the Two Lands; If he sees one who sins with his finger that is, a false scribe, he takes away his provisions by the flood. As for a scribe who sins with his finger, His son will not be enrolled.

33. If you spend your life with these things in your heart, Your children will see them.

## Chapter 16

34. Do not unbalance the scale nor make the weights false, Nor diminish the fractions of the grain measure; Do not wish for the grain measures of the fields And then cast aside those of the treasury. Tehuti sits by the balance, While his heart is the plummet. Where is a spirit as great as knowledge The one who discovered these things, to create them?

35. Do not get for yourself short weights; If you see someone cheating, At a distance you must pass him by. Do not be avaricious for copper, And abjure fine clothes; What good is one cloaked in fine linen woven as mek, When he cheats before Amen. When gold is heaped on gold, At daybreak it turns to lead.

## Chapter 17

36. Beware of robbing the grain measure To falsify its fractions; Do not act wrongfully through force, Although it is empty inside; May you have it measure exactly as to its size, Your hand stretching out with precision.

37. Make not for yourself a measure of two capacities, For then it is toward the depths that you will go. The measure is the reflection of light. Its abomination is the one who takes. As for a grain measurer who multiplies and subtracts, His eye will seal up against him.

38. Do not receive the harvest tax of a cultivator, Nor bind up a papyrus against him to lead him astray. Do not enter into collusion with the grain measurer, Nor play with the seed allotment, More important is the threshing floor for barley Than swearing by the Great Throne.

## Chapter 18

39. Do not go to bed fearing tomorrow, For when day breaks what is tomorrow? Man knows not what tomorrow is! Amen is success, Man is failure. The words which men say pass on one side, The things which Amen does pass on another side.

40. Do not say, "I am without fault," Nor try to seek out trouble. Fault is the business of Amen, It is locked up with his seal.

There is no success in the hand of Amen, Nor is there failure before Him; If he turns himself about to seek out success, In a moment He destroys him.

41. Be strong in your heart, make your mind firm, Do not steer with your tongue; The tongue of a man is the steering oar of a boat, And the Lord of All is its pilot.

## Chapter 19

42. Do not enter the council chamber in the presence of a magistrate And then falsify your speech. Do not go up and down with your accusation When your witnesses stand readied. Do not overstate through oaths in the name of your lord, Through pleas in the place of questioning.

43. Tell the truth before the magistrate, lest he gain power over your body; If you come before him the next day, He will concur with all you say; He will present your case in court before the Council of the Thirty, And it will be lenient another time as well.

## Chapter 20

44. Do not corrupt the people of the law court, Nor put aside the just man, Do not agree because of garments of white, Nor accept one in rags. Take not the gift of the strong man, Nor repress the weak for him. Justice is a wonderful gift of Amen, And He will render it to whomever he wishes. The strength of one like him Saves a poor wretch from his beatings.

45. Do not make false enrollment lists, For they are a serious affair deserving death; They are serious oaths of the kind promising not to misuse an office, And they are to be investigated by an informer.

46. Do not falsify the oracles on a papyrus And (thereby) alter the designs of Amen. Do not arrogate to yourself the might of Amen As if Destiny and Fortune did not exist.

47. Hand property over to its rightful owners, And seek out life for yourself; Let not your heart build in their house, for then your neck will be on the execution block.33

## Chapter 21

48. Do not say, I have found a strong protector And now I can challenge a man in my town. Do not say, I have found an active intercessor, And now I can challenge him whom I hate.

49. Indeed, you cannot know the plans of Amen; You cannot perceive tomorrow. Sit yourself at the hands of Amen; Your tranquility will cause them to open.

50. As for the crocodile deprived of his tongue, the fear of him is negligible. Empty not your soul to everybody And do not diminish thereby your importance; Do not circulate your words to others, Nor fraternize with one who is too candid.

51. Better is a man whose knowledge is inside him Than one who talks to disadvantage. One cannot run to attain perfection; One cannot create only to destroy it.

## Chapter 22

52. Do not castigate your friend in a dispute, And do not let him say his innermost thoughts; Do not fly up to greet him When you do not see how he acts. May you first comprehend his accusation And cool down your opponent.

53. Leave it to him and he will empty his soul; Sleep knows how to find him out; Take his feet, do not bother him; Fear him, do not underestimate him. Indeed, you cannot know the plans of Amen, You cannot perceive tomorrow. Sit yourself at the hands of Amen; Your tranquility will cause them to open.

## Chapter 23

54. Do not eat a meal in the presence of a magistrate, Nor set to speaking first. If you are satisfied with false words, Enjoy yourself with your spittle.

55. Look at the cup in front of you, And let it suffice your need. Even as a noble is important in his office, He is like the abundance of a well when it is drawn.

## Chapter 24

56. Do not listen to the accusation of an official indoors, And then repeat it to another outside. Do not allow your discussions to be brought outside So that your heart will not be grieved.

57. The heart of a man is the voice of his soul, So take care not to slight it; A man who stands at the side of an official Should not have his name known in the street.

## Chapter 25

58. Do not jeer at a blind man nor tease a dwarf, Neither interfere with the condition of a cripple; Do not taunt a man who is in the hand of Amen, Nor scowl at him if he errs.

59. Man is clay and straw, And Amen is his potter; He overthrows and he builds daily, He impoverishes a thousand if He wishes. He makes a thousand into examiners, When He is in His hour of life. How fortunate is he who reaches the Afterlife, When he is safe in the hand of Amen.

## Chapter 26

60. Do not stay in the tavern And join someone greater than you, Whether he be high or low in his station, An old man or a youth; But take as a friend for yourself someone compatible; The sun is helpful though he is far away.

61. When you see someone greater than you outside, And attendants following him, respect him. And give a hand to an old man filled with beer; Respect him as his children would.

62. The strong arm is not weakened when it is uncovered, The back is not broken when one bends it; Better is the poor man who speaks sweet words, Than the rich man who speaks harshly.

63. A pilot who sees into the distance Will not let his ship capsize.

## Chapter 27

64. Do not reproach someone older than you, For he has seen the Sun before you; Do not let yourself be reported to the elders when he rises, With the words, "Another young man has reproached an elder." Very sick in the sight of men is a young man who reproaches an elder.

65. Let him beat you with your hands folded, Let him reproach you while you keep quiet. Then when you come before him in the morning, He will give you bread freely.

## Chapter 28

66. Do not expose a widow if you have caught her in your fields, Nor fail to give way if she is accused. Do not turn a stranger away from your oil jar That it may be made double for your family. Amen loves him who cares for the poor, More than him who respects the wealthy.

## Chapter 29

67. Do not turn people away from crossing the river When you have room in your ferryboat; If a steering oar is given you in the midst of the deep waters, So bend back your hands to take it up. It is not an abomination in the hand of Amen If the passenger is not cared for.

68. Do not acquire a ferryboat on the river, And then attempt to seek out its fares; Take the fare from the man of means, But (also) accept the destitute (without charge).

## Chapter 30

69. Mark for yourself these thirty chapters: They please, they instruct, They are the foremost of all books; They teach the ignorant. If they are read to an ignorant man, He will be purified through them. Seize them; put them in your mind And have men interpret them, explaining as a Nahmir. As to a scribe who is experienced in his position, He will find himself worthy of being Enderase.

It is finished. By the writing of Senu, son of the Righteous father Pamiu.

The Prophecies of Neferti

**THE PROPHECY**

**1. There was a time when the majesty of King Snefru, the justified, was beneficent in this whole land.**

2. On one of those days the magistrates of the residence entered the palace to offer greetings. And they went out having offered greetings in accordance with their daily custom. Then his majesty said to the seal-bearer at his side: "Go, bring me the magistrates of the residence who have gone from here after today's greetings."

3. They were ushered in to him straightaway and were on their bellies before his majesty a second time. His majesty said to them: "Comrades, I have had you summoned in order that you seek out for me a son of yours who is wise, or a brother of yours who excels, or a friend of yours who has done a noble deed, so that he may speak to me some fine words, choice phrases at the hearing of which my majesty may be entertained."

4. They were on their bellies before his majesty once more. Then they spoke before his majesty: "There is a great rector-priest of Bastet, O king, our lord, Neferti by name. He is a citizen with valiant arm, a scribe excellent with his fingers, a gentleman of greater wealth than any peer of his. May he be brought for your majesty to see!" Said his majesty: "Go, bring him to me!" He was ushered in to him straightaway, and he was on his belly before his majesty.

5. His majesty said: "Come, Neferti, my friend, speak to me some fine words, choice phrases at the hearing of which my majesty may be entertained!" Said the rector-priest Neferti: "Of what has happened or of what will happen, O king, my lord?" Said his majesty: "Of what will happen. As soon as today is here, it is passed over." He stretched out his hand to a box of writing equipment, took scroll and palette and began to put into writing the words of the rector-priest Neferti, that wise man of the East, servant of Bastet in her East, and native of the nome of On.

6. As he deplored what had happened in the land, evoked the state of the East, with Asiatics roaming in their strength, frightening those about to harvest and seizing cattle from the plough, he said: Stir, my heart, Bewail this land, from which you have sprung! When there is silence before evil, And when what should be chided is feared, Then the great man is overthrown in the land of your birth. Tire not while this is before you.

7. Rise against what is before you! Lo, the great no longer rule the land, What was made has been unmade, Ra should begin to recreate! The land is quite perished, no remnant is left, Not the black of a nail is spared from its fate. Yet while the land suffers, none care for it, None speak, none shed tears: "How fares this land!" The sun disk, covered, shines not for people to see, One cannot live when clouds conceal, All are numb from lack of it.

8. I will describe what is before me, I do not foretell what does not come: Dry is the river of Kemit, One crosses the water on foot; One seeks water for ships to sail on, Its course having turned into shore land. Shore land will turn into water, Watercourse back into shore land. South wind will combat north wind, Sky will lack the single wind.

9. A strange bird will breed in the Delta marsh, Having made its nest beside the people, The people having let it approach by default. Then perish those delightful things, The fishponds full of fish-eaters, Teeming with fish and fowl. All happiness has vanished, The land is bowed down in distress, Owing to those feeders, Asiatics who roam the land. Foes have risen in the East, Asiatics have come down to Kemit. If the fortress is crowded Desert flocks will drink at the river of Kemit, Take their ease on the shores for lack of one to fear For this land is to-and-fro, knowing not what comes, What-will-be being hidden according as one says: "When sight and hearing fail the mute leads." I show you the land in turmoil, What should not be has come to pass. Men will seize weapons of warfare, The land will live in uproar. Men will make arrows of copper, Will crave blood for bread, Will laugh aloud at distress. None will weep over death, None will wake fasting for death, Each man's heart is for himself. Mourning is not done today, Hearts have quite abandoned it. A man sits with his back turned, While one slays another. I show you the son as enemy, the brother as foe, A man slaying his father.

10. Every mouth is full of "how I wish" All happiness has vanished; The land is ruined, its fate decreed, Deprived of produce, lacking in crops, What was made has been unmade. One seizes a man's goods, gives them to an outsider, I show you the master in need, the outsider stated, The lazy stuffs himself, the active is needy. One gives only with hatred, To silence the mouth that speaks; To answer a speech the arm thrusts a stick One speaks by killing him. Speech falls on the heart like fire, One cannot endure the word of mouth.

11. The land is shrunk, its rulers are many, It is bare, its taxes are great; The grain is low, the measure is large, It is measured to overflowing. Ra will withdraw from mankind: Though he will rise at his hour, One will not know when noon has come; No one will discern his shadow, No face will be dazzled by seeing him, No eyes will moisten with water. He will be in the sky like the moon, His nightly course unchanged, His rays on the face as before.

12. I show you the land in turmoil: The weak-armed is strong-armed, One salutes him who saluted. I show you the undermost uppermost, What was fumed on the back turns the belly. Men will live in the graveyard, The beggar will gain riches, The great will rob to live. The poor will eat bread, Gone from the earth is the nome of On, The birthplace of every Neter.

13. Then a king will come from the South, Justified, by name, Son of a woman of Ta-Seti, child of Upper Egypt. He will take the white crown, He will wear the red crown; He will join the Two Mighty Ones, He will please the Two Lords with what they wish, With field-circler in his fist, oar in his grasp. Rejoice, O people of his time, The son of man will make his name for all eternity! The evil-minded, the treason-plotters, They suppress their speech in fear of him; Asiatics will fall to his sword, Libyans will fall to his flame, Rebels to his wrath, traitors to his might, As the wisdom on his brow subdues the rebels for him. One will build the Walls-of-the-Ruler, To bar Asiatics from entering Kemit; They will beg water as supplicants, So as to let their cattle drink. Then Order will return to its seat, While Chaos is driven away. Rejoice he who may see, he who may attend the king! And he who is wise will libate for me, When he sees fulfilled what I have spoken!

It is finished.

**Papyrus of Moral precepts**
32nd Dynasty – ca. 305 BCE

1. Make it not in a heart of a mother to enter into bitterness. Kill not, nor expose yourself to be killed, Make not a companion of a wicked man, it is an abomination. Do not do after the advice of a fool, Do not abuse or relinquish your children till they are old, and have increased in age and strength.

2. May it not happen to you to maltreat an inferior, and may it happen to you to respect the venerable, May it not happen to you to maltreat your wife whose strength is less than yours, but may she find in you a protector, Do not curse him who helps you, May it not happen to you to cause your infant to suffer, if he is weak, (on the contrary) assist him, Do not abandon one son to another of your sons, who is stronger or more courageous, Do not amuse yourself or play on those who are dependent on you, Do not allow your son to be familiar with a married woman.

3. Do not pervert the heart of your acquaintance, if he is pure. Do not take a haughty attitude.

4. Truth is sent by Amen.

5. Even if he were an important person, a man whose nature is evil does not know how to remain upright.

6. Celebrate the feast of Amen and begin it at the correct time. It is unpleasant in the land when Amen if forgotten.

7. Be careful to avoid the mistake of lying: it will prevent you from fighting the torment inside yourself.

8. Choose what is good to say and keep bad words prisoner in your body.

9. Keep a loving heart whose words stay hidden. Amen will provide for your needs. Amen listens to what you say; your offering of prayer will be acceptable enough.

10. Everyone can master their own nature if the wisdom which he has been taught has made that nature stable.

11. A lazy man never gets around to doing anything. He who knows how to make plans is worthy of consideration.

12. Do not join a crowd that you meet when it has gathered to fight. Keep away from rebels.

13. Give back in abundance the bread your mother gave you. Support her as she supported you.

14. Pour out the water of libation for your father and mother who rest in the valley of death. The ancestors will bear witness to this just act.

15. Scorn the woman who has a bad reputation in your town; do not look at her as she passes. Do not try to sleep with her.

16. Marry a woman when you are young, and let her have children while you are young, all will go well for the man whose household is numerous.

17. Distance yourself from the rebel; do not make a friend of him. Make friends with the just and righteous man whose actions you have observed.

18. Build your own home for yourself and do not assume that your parent's house will come to you by right.

19. Do not eat bread without giving some to those near you who do not have anything to eat, since the bread is eternal while man does not last.

20. Do not sit down when there is a person standing who is older than you or whose rank is higher than yours.

21. You will know happiness if your life is lived within the limits set by the will of Amen.

22. Do not fill your heart with desire for the goods of others, but rather concern yourself with what you have built up yourself.

23. When death comes, it embraces the old like a child in the arms of its mother.

24. Do not lose yourself in the exterior world to the extent that you neglect the place of your eternal rest.

It is finished from beginning to end, as it was found in writing.

# Proverbs Attested from the Temple of Amen of Ipet-isut (Called Karnak)
## *ca.* 1391–1351 BCE

**From the Outer Temple**

1. **The best and shortest road towards knowledge of truth is Nature.**

2. For every joy there is a price to be paid.

3. If his heart rules him, his conscience will soon take the place of the rod.

4. What you are doing does not matter so much as what you are learning from doing it. · *It is better not to know and to know that one does not know*, than presumptuously to attribute some random meaning to symbols.

5. If you search for the *laws of harmony*, you will find *knowledge*.

6. If you are searching for a *Neter*, observe *Nature*!

7. Exuberance is a good stimulus towards action, but the inner light grows in silence and concentration.

8. Not the greatest Master can go even one step for his disciple; in himself he must experience each stage of developing consciousness. Therefore he will *know* nothing for which he is not ripe.

9. The body is the house of Amen. That is why it is said, "Man know yourself."

10. True teaching is not an accumulation of knowledge; it is an awaking of consciousness which goes through successive stages.

11. The man who knows how to lead one of his brothers towards what he has known may one day be saved by that very brother.

12. People bring about their own undoing through their tongues.

13. If one tries to navigate unknown waters one runs the risk of shipwreck. Leave him in error who loves his error.

14. Every man is rich in excuses to safeguard *his* prejudices, *his* instincts, and *his* opinions.

15. To know means to record in one's memory; but to understand means to blend with the thing and to assimilate it in oneself.

42

16. There are two kinds of error: *blind credulity* and *piecemeal criticism*. Never believe a word without putting its truth to the test; discernment does not grow in laziness; and this faculty of discernment is indispensable to the Seeker. Sound skepticism is the necessary condition for good discernment; but *piecemeal criticism is an error.*

17. Love is one thing, knowledge is another.

18. True sages are those who give what they have, without meanness and without secret!

19. An answer brings no illumination unless the question has matured to a point where it gives rise to this answer which so becomes its fruit. Therefore learn how to put a question.

20. What reveals itself to me ceases to be mysterious—for me alone; if I unveil it to anyone else, he hears mere words which betray the living sense; Profanation, but never revelation.

21. The first concerning the 'secrets': *all cognition comes from inside*; we are therefore initiated only by ourselves, but the Master gives the keys.

22. The second concerning the 'way': the seeker has need of a Master to guide him and lift him up when he falls, to lead him back to the right way when he strays.

23. Understanding develops by degrees.

24. As to deserving, know that the gift of Heaven is free; this gift of Knowledge is so great that no effort whatever could hope to 'deserve' it.

25. If the Master teaches what is error, the disciple's submission is slavery; if he teaches truth, this submission is ennoblement.

26. There grows no wheat where there is no grain.

27. The only thing that is humiliating is helplessness.

1. **From the Inner Temple**

2. An answer is profitable in proportion to the intensity of the quest.

3. Listen to your conviction, even if they seem absurd to your reason.

4. Know the world in yourself. Never look for yourself in the world, for this would be to project your illusion.

5. To teach one must know the nature of those whom one is teaching.

6. In every vital activity it is the path that matters.

7. The way of knowledge is narrow.

8. Each truth you learn will be, for you, as new as if it had never been written.

9. The only active force that arises out of possession is fear of losing the object of possession.

10. If you defy an enemy by doubting his courage you double it.

11. The nut doesn't reveal the tree it contains.

12. For knowledge ... you should know that peace is an indispensable condition of getting it.

13. The first thing necessary in teaching is a master; the second is a pupil capable of carrying on the tradition.

14. Peace is the fruit of activity, not of sleep.

15. Envious greed must govern to possess and ambition must possess to govern.

16. When the governing class isn't chosen for quality it is chosen for material wealth: this always means decadence, the lowest stage a society can reach.

17. Two tendencies govern human choice and effort, the search after quantity and the search after quality. They classify mankind. Some follow Ma'at, others seek the way of animal instinct.

18. Qualities of a moral order are measured by deeds.

19. One foot isn't enough to walk with.

20. Our senses serve to affirm, not to know.

21. We mustn't confuse mastery with mimicry, knowledge with superstitious ignorance.

22. Physical consciousness is indispensable for the achievement of knowledge.

23. A man can't be the judge of his neighbor's intelligence. His own vital experience is never his neighbor's.

24. No discussion can throw light if it wanders from the real point.

25. Your body is the temple of knowledge.

26. Experience will show you, a Master can only point the way.

27. A house has the character of the man who lives in it.

28. All organs work together in the functioning of the whole.

29. A man's heart is his own Neter.

30. A pupil may show you by his own efforts how much he deserves to learn from you.

31. Routine and prejudice distort vision. Each man thinks his own horizon is the limit of the world.

32. You will free yourself when you learn to be neutral and follow the instructions of your heart without letting things perturb you. This is the way of Ma'at.

33. Judge by cause, not by effect.

34. Growth in consciousness doesn't depend on the will of the intellect or its possibilities but on the intensity of the inner urge.

35. Every man must act in the rhythm of his time ... such is wisdom.

36. Men need images. Lacking them they invent idols. Better then to found the images on realities that lead the true seeker to the source.

37. Ma'at, who links universal to terrestrial, the divine with the human is incomprehensible to the cerebral intelligence.

38. Have the wisdom to abandon the values of a time that has passed and pick out the constituents of the future. An environment must be suited to the age and men to their environment.

39. Everyone finds himself in the world where he belongs. The essential thing is to have a fixed point from which to check its reality now and then.

40. Always watch and follow nature.

41. A phenomenon always arises from the interaction of complementaries. If you want something look for the complement that will elicit it. Set causes Heru. Heru redeems Set.

42. All seed answer light, but the color is different.

43. The plant reveals what is in the seed.

44. Popular beliefs on essential matters must be examined in order to discover the original thought.

45. It is the passive resistance from the helm that steers the boat.

46. The key to all problems is the problem of consciousness.

47. Man must learn to increase his sense of responsibility and of the fact that everything he does will have its consequences.

48. If you would build something solid, don't work with wind; always look for a fixed point, something you know that is stable ... yourself.

49. If you would know yourself, take yourself as starting point and go back to its source; your beginning will disclose your end.

50. Images are nearer reality than cold definitions.

51. Seek peacefully, you will find.

52. Organization is impossible unless those who know the laws of harmony lay the foundation.

53. It is no use whatever preaching Wisdom to men; you must inject it into their blood.

54. Knowledge is consciousness of reality. Reality is the sum of the laws that govern nature and of the causes from which they flow.

55. Social good is what brings peace to family and society.

56. Knowledge is not necessarily wisdom.

57. By knowing one reaches belief. By doing one gains conviction. When you know, dare.

58. Altruism is the mark of a superior being.

59. All is within yourself. Know your most inward self and look for what corresponds with it in nature.

60. The seed cannot sprout upwards without simultaneously sending roots into the ground.

61. The seed includes all the *possibilities* of the tree. ... The seed will develop these possibilities, however, only if it receives corresponding energies from the sky.

62. Grain must return to the earth, die, and decompose for new growth to begin.

63. Man, know yourself ... and you will know Amen.

### Readiness or preparedness for admittance

1. Control of thought.

2. Control of action, or ***Justice*** (i.e., the unswerving righteousness of thought and action).

3. Steadfastness of purpose, or ***Fortitude***.

4. Identity with spiritual life, or higher ideals (i.e., ***Temperance*** which is an attribute attained when the individual had gained conquest over the passionate nature).

5. Evidence of having a mission in life.

6. Evidence of a call to spiritual Orders of the Priesthood in the teachings; the combination of which was equivalent to ***Prudence*** or a deep insight and graveness that befitted the faculty of seership.

7. Freedom from resentment, when under the experience of persecution and wrong. This was known as courage.

8. Confidence in the power of the master as teacher.

9. Confidence in one's own ability to learn; both attributes being known as fidelity.

## Original Kemetic Proverbs

1. The tail of the dog never get straight even if you set a mold for it.
2. A monkey is a gazelle in its mother's eyes.
3. One never changes.
4. An absent person has his excuse.
5. Borrowing is bad, and returning money is a loss.
6. Time never gets tired of Running.
7. Bathe her and then look at her.
8. Be patient with a bad neighbor. Maybe he'll leave or a disaster will take him out.
9. Cover your candle, it will light more.
10. Dress up a stick and it'll be a beautiful wife.
11. He who couldn't overcome the donkey took on the saddle.
12. He whose house is made out of glass, shouldn't throw stones at people.
13. If your friend is (like) honey, don't lick it all.
14. If you marry a monkey for his wealth, the money goes and the monkey remains as is.
15. Knowledge is in the head, not the copybook.
16. News that's for money today will be for free tomorrow.
17. Stretch your legs as far as your quilt goes.
18. This cub is from that lion.
19. What comes easily is lost easily.

20. When I hear you, I believe you. When I see what you do, I'm surprised.

21. When the Neteru arrive, the devils leave.

22. Give saturday, you will find Sunday .

23. Give me a fish, I have the day's food. Teach me how to fish and I will have everyday's food.

24. The man a bald woman got will be easily seduced by a woman with beautiful hair.

25. He kills the victim and walks in his funeral.

26. Lying has no legs.

27. Learn politeness from the impolite.

28. Making money selling manure is better than losing money selling musk.

29. Malice drinks its own poison.

30. Pride goes before destruction, and a haughty spirit before a fall.

31. Put a rope around your neck and many will be happy to drag you along.

32. Put by for a rainy day.

33. Run as hard as a wild beast if you will, but you won't get any reward greater than that destined for you.

34. The barking of a dog does not disturb the man on a camel.

35. The tyrant is only the slave turned inside out.

36. A beautiful thing is never perfect.

37. A man's ruin lies in his tongue.

www.ingramcontent.com/pod-product-compliance
Lightning Source LLC
Chambersburg PA
CBHW030928090426
42737CB00007B/359